A PARALLEL PRESS CHAPBOOK

AMERICA'S FOUNDERS

JAMES MADISON

Champion of Liberty and Justice

JOHN P. KAMINSKI

PARALLEL PRESS · 2006

ISBN 1-893311-65-1
America's Founders is a chapbook series published by Parallel Press, an imprint of the University of Wisconsin–Madison Libraries, in collaboration with the Center for the Study of the American Constitution, in the Department of History at the University of Wisconsin–Madison.

http://parallelpress.library.wisc.edu

FIRST EDITION

The America's Founders series is dedicated to the several hundred Mentor Teachers who are the heart and soul of the Center for Civic Education's program "We the People: The Citizen and the Constitution."

This chapbook is dedicated to

DREW HORVATH
Lawrence Central High School
Indianapolis, Indiana

REBECCA REEDER
Aboite Elementary School
Fort Wayne, Indiana

LYNNETTE WALLACE
Canterbury Middle School
Fort Wayne, Indiana

THE AMERICAN POLITICAL SYSTEM IS A COMPLEX LABYRINTH that has survived for over 200 years. Surprisingly, it was a short, shy, soft-spoken, scholar-like man, who, more than any other person, laid the foundations of this complicated system. For his contributions, James Madison has been called the Father of the Constitution. Madison, however, always shared credit for writing the Constitution. "This was not, like the fabled Goddess of Wisdom, the offspring of a single brain. It ought to be regarded as the work of many heads and many hands."*

Born in 1751, Madison called himself "a child of the Revolution." Although commissioned a colonel in the Virginia militia, he never served in the military. His battlefields were the legislative and convention chambers. His weapons were not muskets and sabers, but words and ideas.** His object was not to win a particular battle or defeat a specific enemy but to champion liberty and justice whenever endangered.

Throughout his lifetime, and throughout American historiography, Madison has been accused of inconsistency—of being an arch nationalist in the 1780s, of opposing and then advocating a federal bill of rights, of being a states rightist during the 1790s, of being a pragmatist while in power during the first two decades of the nine-

---

* Madison to William Cogswell, March 10, 1814, *Madison Papers*, Library of Congress.

** In *The Federalist* 37, Madison wrote of the importance of words in expressing ideas. "The use of words is to express ideas. Perspicuity therefore requires not only that the ideas should be distinctly formed, but that they should be expressed by words distinctly and exclusively appropriated to them. But no language is so copious as to supply words and phrases for every complex idea, or so correct as not to include many equivocally denoting different ideas." Even "When the Almighty himself condescends to address mankind in their own language, his meaning, luminous as it must be, is rendered dim and doubtful, by the cloudy medium through which it is communicated."

teenth century, and finally of opposing states rightists during the last decade and a half of his life. In reality, however, Madison was consistent. His focus was never on a particular type of government per se. Whenever he saw liberty and justice threatened by a "change of circumstances," he sought means to limit or eliminate the danger.

Madison first saw the danger to liberty and justice in colonial Virginia when Baptist ministers were imprisoned "for publishing their religious Sentiments." He strongly opposed such oppression publicly, and as a political neophyte he worked in the Virginia convention of June 1776 to broaden the religious toleration advocated by George Mason to full freedom of religion. He strongly opposed the new British imperial policy implemented by various ministries after 1763 and joined the movement for independence in the early 1770s. When he saw the danger posed by the states to liberty and justice, he advocated the reduction of state power and the enhancement of federal authority under the Articles of Confederation. When the vices of the state and Confederation governments became apparent and seemingly incapable of being changed within the existing federal arrangement, he sought, through the construction of a new system of government, to achieve liberty, justice, and happiness for his fellow citizens. When Secretary of the Treasury Alexander Hamilton and later the Federalist Party and the federal judiciary threatened liberty and justice through a "forced construction" of the Constitution, Madison argued in the Virginia Resolutions of 1798 for a reduction of federal authority and the empowerment of state legislatures in their relationship with the federal government. When the Jeffersonian Republicans assumed power after the Revolution of 1800, Madison adopted a more pragmatic attitude toward the federal government. Finally, during his retirement years, Madison opposed the neo-Antifederalists who supported states rights as a means of preserving their slavery-based culture and economy.

Throughout the 1780s Madison looked to the state courts for protection from oppressive state legislatures. During the debate over ratifying the new U.S. Constitution, Madison predicted that the federal judiciary would protect liberty and justice from oppression from both state and federal governments. In 1789 he proposed the bill of rights as a weapon to be used by federal courts to defend liberty and justice. In the late 1790s, however, Madison looked to the states for protection from the federal judiciary, which was being used as a partisan instrument of oppression. But Madison believed that the Supreme Court under Chief Justice John Marshall "naturally and liberally" interpreted the Constitution to give the federal government the kind of power envisioned by the Federal Convention of 1787 and by Federalists in the ratification debate that followed. Only in the 1819 case of *McCulloch* v. *Maryland* did Madison believe that Marshall's court had gone too far with a "forced construction" in expanding the implied powers of the Constitution.

Throughout his long years of service, James Madison worked to defend liberty and justice. Sometimes this required him to emphasize local or state power, sometimes federal power. But he always wanted power to serve the cause of freedom. Thus, in looking at Madison's defense of liberty and justice from wherever danger appeared, we see a remarkable consistency.

• • • • • • •

This chapbook is dedicated to three Indiana teachers—one each in a high school, a middle school, and an elementary school. Drew Horvath, Rebecca Reeder, and Lynnette Wallace are three of the great mentor teachers associated with the Center for Civic Education. They are all extremely well read in the constitutional history of our country and are all simply fantastic, dedicated teachers.

Drew is in many ways still a student. His appetite for knowledge—especially knowledge that he can transmit to his students—is unquenchable. He couples a sort of boyish innocence with a profound appreciation for the problems faced throughout our history as well as the ongoing problems we face in our present-day world. He never ceases to ask questions. He is a free spirit in and out of the classroom, whether that be moving the first-down chains at the home games of the Indianapolis Colts, taking his students to the national finals in Washington, D.C., or instructing civics teachers in Bosnia. To see the affection and enthusiasm he evokes from his students is a joy. Rebecca is a no-nonsense, dedicated teacher. Ever since she can remember, she has always wanted to be a teacher. She did that first with her two sons, and then she went into the classroom in Fort Wayne. She has the long-range good of her students at heart—she wants to see each student achieve their fullest potential. In particular, she has worked hard to develop opportunities for gifted students. She is a remarkable leader and administrator, as I have seen first-hand, watching her adeptly direct summer teacher institutes. Lynnette is a bubbly, effervescent person. She makes all those she comes in contact with feel good—especially her students. She is a gifted novelist and sports enthusiast. She is sensitive and thoughtful and has gained the respect and admiration of her colleagues in Fort Wayne and throughout the country.

Each of these extraordinary teachers is special to me. It is a joy and an inspiration to be around them and to see how they interact with their students, their fellow mentor teachers, and their fellow teachers whom they have guided so expertly. They are remarkable human beings.

INTRODUCTION

James Madison entered the national political scene at the end of the War for Independence. Throughout the 1780s he steadily advocated increased powers for Congress under the Articles of Confederation—America's first federal constitution. When it became evident that amendments to the Articles could not be obtained, Madison worked outside of the normal political and constitutional arenas to obtain change.

At the Federal Convention that met in Philadelphia from May through September 1787, Madison was arguably the most influential delegate. He advocated radical alterations both in the structure of the country's constitution and in the relationship between the central government and the states. Madison based his proposals upon (1) his own comprehensive study of the history of confederacies and why they had always failed, (2) his thorough analysis of the weaknesses of Congress and the vices of the states under the Articles of Confederation, (3) his years of studying history, political science, and human nature, and (4) his years of service in Congress and the Virginia House of Delegates.

Madison's contribution to the American political system did not end with the promulgation of the Constitution in September 1787. He became the most important Federalist in the struggle to ratify the Constitution—serving as a clearinghouse of information in New York City, as a co-author of the monumental *"Federalist Papers,"* and as the Federalist champion in the Virginia ratifying convention in June 1788, where he successfully battled the renowned Patrick Henry and the revered George Mason.

Denied election to the first U.S. Senate by Patrick Henry's dominance in the Virginia legislature (state legislatures elected U.S. senators until 1913), Madison was elected to the first U.S. House of Representatives. He wrote President George Washington's first inaugural address, and, for two years, Madison served as de facto prime minister, leading the first federal Congress in putting muscle and fiber on the skeletal Constitution. He also virtually single-handedly led the struggle to add a bill of rights to the Constitution.

After two years, however, Madison and his longtime political collaborator and friend Secretary of State Thomas Jefferson became increasingly disenchanted with the policies of Secretary of the Treasury Alexander Hamilton. To combat the pro-British, pro-Northern, monarchical tendencies of Hamilton, Madison and Jefferson organized an opposition political party. The first American political party system emerged, and a loyal opposition arose to defend liberty from perceived threats.

Contemporaries recognized Madison's political genius, but they disagreed on whether he was pragmatic or impractical. Massachusetts Representative Fisher Ames felt that Madison was "too much attached to his theories, for a politician." Although choosing politics as his profession, Madison, according to Ames, thought of it as "rather a science, than a business with him. He adopts his maxims as he finds them in books, and with too little regard to the actual state of things."[1] Hamilton referred to Madison as "a clever man," but too "little Acquainted with the world."[2]

Madison left Congress in 1797. Working from Virginia, Madison helped Jefferson to achieve the "Revolution of 1800" in which President John Adams and the Federalist Party were defeated. Madison served as Jefferson's secretary of state for eight years during which

1. Fisher Ames to George Richards Minot, New York, May 29, 1789, Charlene Bangs Bickford et al., eds., *Documentary History of the First Federal Congress: Correspondence* (Baltimore, 2004), XV, 651.

2. Conversation with George Beckwith, New York, October 1789, Harold C. Syrett, ed., *The Papers of Alexander Hamilton* (27 vols., New York, 1961–1987), V, 488.

he experienced the highs of acquiring the vast Louisiana Territory that doubled the size of the United States and the lows of an increasingly hostile domestic response to the administration's inability to combat British and French depredations on the high seas. Madison succeeded Jefferson as president and stumblingly led the country to war with Britain. Peace found the beleaguered president riding a wave of nationalistic pride that raised his popularity. As the country united and partisanship waned, Madison retired to Montpelier, his Virginia Piedmont plantation, where he lived until 1836, as one of the last surviving leaders of the Revolutionary era.

EARLY LIFE

James Madison was born on the Virginia Piedmont at Port Conway, King George County, on March 16, 1751, on his grandmother's ancestral plantation. Four generations earlier, his father's ancestors had emigrated to Virginia, acquiring a sizeable tract of land through Virginia's generous "headright" system.[3] Madison's grandfather, Ambrose, moved his family to Orange County. His plantation of over 3,000 acres was perfectly situated. The virgin red soil was rich, the temperatures moderate, and, unlike the Tidewater, the location was healthy. Located between the Southeast Mountains to the east and the majestic Blue Ridge Mountains, about thirty miles to the west, the plantation had gently-rolling fertile arable land, good pasture, valuable timber stands, and numerous streams (called runs) and springs. Not to be named *Montpelier* until around 1780, this would be the only home that James Madison would ever know.

Ambrose Madison died in 1732 and left his estate to his son, who was only nine years old. The plantation was run by Ambrose's widow, Frances Taylor Madison, until her son, James Madison Sr. reached age eighteen. James Sr. married Nelly Conway in September 1749. Just seventeen, Nelly was the youngest daughter of a merchant-planter of Caroline County. By 1757, the plantation had grown to over 4,000 acres and James Sr. was among the most prominent planters in Orange County. By 1782, the family owned at least 118 slaves. James Sr. built the mansion house at its present location in 1759 and presided over

3. Each person emigrating to Virginia was given fifty acres of land. Those paying the way for other immigrants to Virginia were also given fifty acres for each person sponsored.

Montpelier until his death in 1801 at the age of 78. His widow, James Madison Jr.'s mother, resided at Montpelier until her death at the age of 98 in 1829.

Like most children in colonial America, James Jr. learned to read and write from his mother and grandmother. His early education at home probably included instruction from the local Anglican minister. A major turning point in James's life occurred when in June 1762 he was sent seventy miles away to a boarding school in King and Queen County operated by Donald Robertson, a forty-five-year-old Scottish immigrant who had been educated at Aberdeen and the University of Edinburgh. Madison was resident in the school for five years. He would later write of Robertson, "all that I have in life I owe largely to that man."[4]

Madison left Robertson's school at the age of sixteen. He returned to Montpelier where he was given more advanced personal instruction by the Reverend Thomas Martin, the newly appointed rector of Madison's home church. Martin had graduated from the College of New Jersey in 1762 and now took up residence at Montpelier where he instructed all of the Madison children. It was through the influence of Martin that Madison decided to attend the College of New Jersey (Princeton) instead of the College of William and Mary, the customary choice of young Virginia gentlemen. The location of William and Mary in the sickly Tidewater, and the recent arrival of the Reverend John Witherspoon as the president of Princeton, also helped Madison decide to go north.

In the summer of 1769 a frail, eighteen-year-old bookish James Madison arrived in Princeton, N.J., and for the next three years he lived in Nassau Hall, the "convenient, airy, and spacious" three-story stone building that served as both a residence hall and classroom building.

4. Quoted in Ralph Ketcham, *James Madison: A Biography* (Charlottesville, Va., 1990), 21.

Madison easily passed the freshman exam and accelerated through the three-year program in two years, graduating in September 1771. Madison was a serious student. His mentor, President John Witherspoon, said of him that "during the whole time he was under [my] tuition, [I] never knew him to do nor to say an improper thing." His studies consumed most of his time and energy. "His only relaxation from study consisted in walking and conversation."[5] After graduating and still unclear as to what his future career would be, Madison continued studying with Witherspoon. Throughout his years at Princeton, but especially during the last eighteen months, Madison was immersed in the history and literature of seventeenth-century England with its epic struggle between king and parliament, and the increasingly angry debate between the American colonies and parliament. Witherspoon, the teacher, taught Madison to be a deep-thinking scholar. Madison left Princeton never wanting to "intoxicate his brain with Idleness & dissipation."[6] Witherspoon, the revolutionary (he signed the Declaration of Independence for New Jersey), taught Madison to be the patriot, supporting America's cause against parliament. The College of New Jersey not only made Madison into a scholar, but prepared him to be a revolutionary and a statesman.

While at Princeton, Madison remained frail. Periodically he suffered from the bilious lax, an intestinal disorder that would probably be diagnosed today as irritable bowel syndrome. This chronic ailment also aggravated his serious condition of hemorrhoids. Since his early youth he also seemed to be plagued by what was called epileptoid hysteria. Madison described the condition as "a constitutional liability to sudden attacks, some-

5. Benjamin Rush to his son James Rush, May 25, 1802, Rush Papers, Library Company of Philadelphia.

6. Madison to William Bradford, Orange, June 10, 1773, William T. Hutchinson et al., eds., *The Papers of James Madison* (Chicago and Charlottesville, 1962–), I, 89.

what resembling Epilepsy, and suspending the intellectual functions. They continued thro' life, with prolonged intervals." It was this ailment that kept him off ships for fear that sailing would bring on attacks.[7] Throughout his youth, Madison looked pale, feeble, and chronically ill. As a young man, Madison expected not to have "a long or healthy life."[8] This sense of foreboding pervaded his thinking as he finished his formal education and returned to Virginia.

A REVOLUTIONARY PUBLIC SERVANT

Although Madison thought about political matters, he did "not meddle with Politicks."[9] He determined "to read Law occasionally and . . . procured books for that purpose."[10] He pictured the law, medicine, and commerce as "honorable and usefull professions"; but, still, he remained uncertain about his future. The law, he wrote, "alone can bring into use many parts of knowledge . . . & pay you for cultivating the Arts of Eloquence. It is a sort of General Lover that woos all the Muses and Graces. This cannot be said so truly of commerce and Physic."[11] He found himself fascinated by "the principles & Modes of Government [which] are too important to be disregarded by an Inquisitive mind and I think are well worthy [of] a critical examination by all students that have health

7. Madison wrote Jefferson on April 27, 1785, that he did not want to cross the Atlantic because it "would be unfriendly to a singular disease of my constitution." Ibid., VIII, 270.

8. Madison to William Bradford, Orange, November 9, 1772, ibid., I, 75.

9. Madison to William Bradford, Orange, September 23, 1773, ibid., I, 97.

10. Madison to William Bradford, Orange, December 1, 1771, ibid., I, 100.

11. Madison to William Bradford, Orange, September 25, 1783, ibid., I, 96.

& Leisure."[12] He spent much of his time reading and thinking—what he called "my customary enjoyments [of] Solitude and Contemplation."[13] Teaching his younger siblings took up only a small amount of his time.

One of Madison's first forays into politics occurred in January 1774 after hearing about the imprisonment of several Baptist ministers in adjacent Culpeper County. They were charged with "publishing their religious Sentiments" without getting a license from the established Anglican Church. Appalled at these violations of the free exercise of religion, Madison "squabbled and scolded, abused and ridiculed so long about it, to so little purpose that I am without common patience."[14] He was pleased that petitions "were forming among the Persecuted Baptists and I fancy it is in the thoughts of the Presbyterians also to intercede for greater liberty in matters of Religion." Madison, however, was pessimistic about liberalizing the official government policy toward dissident religions. "Incredible and extravagant stories" about religious "Enthusiasm" had been propagated in the legislature, making any kind of reform doubtful. That was indeed unfortunate for Virginia, because Madison firmly believed that "Religious bondage shackles and debilitates the mind and unfits it for every noble enterprize, every expanded prospect."[15] This early encounter with religious persecution inspired Madison. Throughout his life, he would be an enemy to violations of personal rights. His outrage now energized him and perhaps gave a turn to his career.

12. Madison to William Bradford, Orange, December 1, 1773, ibid., I, 101.

13. Madison to William Bradford, Orange, July 1, 1774, ibid., I, 114.

14. Madison to William Bradford, Orange, January 24, 1774, ibid., I, 106.

15. Madison to William Bradford, Orange, April 1, 1774, ibid., I, 112–13.

In April 1774, Madison accompanied his younger brother William to Princeton where he was enrolled in Princeton's prep school. While in Philadelphia, Madison heard about parliament's draconian response to the Boston Tea Party. The merciless closing of the port of Boston, the suspension of the colony's charter, the suspension of the civil government, and the appointment of a military governor seemed to be disproportionately harsh and a gross attack on the liberty of the colony. Madison and other Virginians joined with Americans from every colony in denouncing this outrageous, despotic legislation. Virginians, Madison wrote, "are willing to fall in with the Other Colonies in any expedient measure, even if that should be the universal prohibition of Trade."[16] They all sensed that some day parliament's tyranny might one day be applied to their own colony.

Madison advocated immediate action, instead of waiting for the British response to American petitions protesting the imperial policies. "Would it not be advisable," he argued, "as soon as possible to begin our defence & to let its continuance or cessation depend on the success of a petition to his majesty. Delay on our part emboldens our adversaries and improves their schemes, whilst it abates the ardor of the Americans inspired with recent Injuries and affords opportunity to our secret enemies to disseminate discord & disunion."[17] Madison felt that "the frequent Assaults that have been made on America, Boston especially, will in the end prove of real advantage."[18]

The Intolerable Acts, as Americans referred to them, were but the final actions in the new imperial policy aimed at gaining greater control over Britain's American colonies. In reality, Madison and other colonists saw the dispute with parliament as a confrontation over the prin-

16. Madison to William Bradford, Orange, July 1, 1774, ibid., I, 115.

17. Madison to William Bradford, Orange, August 23, 1774, ibid., I, 121.

18. Madison to William Bradford, Virginia, January 24, 1774, ibid., I, 105.

ciple of self-government, the essence of liberty. Americans since their settlement had exercised a significant amount of self-rule. But according to parliament, any authority exercised by the colonies was a grant from the king and parliament that could be revoked at the will of the imperial authority. The Declaratory Act, passed in 1766 a day after parliament repealed the hated Stamp Act, proclaimed parliament's unalterable position that it could bind Americans "in all cases whatsoever." Much of Madison's future career would center over these very same issues of the division of power between federal and state governments.

In December 1774 Madison was elected to the Orange County Committee of Safety, which was charged with enforcing the Continental Association established by the First Continental Congress. The Association prohibited most colonial exportations and importations in an attempt to pressure British economic interests to lobby parliament to change its policies toward America. Madison described the Revolutionary fervor mounting in Virginia.

> The proceedings of the Congress are universally approved of in this Province & I am persuaded will be faithfully adhered to. A spirit of Liberty & Patriotism animates all degrees and denominations of men. Many publicly declare themselves ready to join the Bostonians as soon as violence is offered them or resistance thought expedient. In many counties independent companies are forming and voluntarily subjecting themselves to military discipline that they may be expert & prepared against a time of Need. I hope it will be a general thing *thro'ought* this province. Such firm and provident steps will either intimidate our enemies or enable us to defy them.[19]

19. Madison to William Bradford, Virginia, November 26, 1774, ibid., I, 129.

In October 1775 Madison was commissioned a colonel in the Orange County militia. His poor health, however, kept him from military service.

In the spring of 1776 Madison was elected to the Virginia provincial convention, the effective ruling authority in Virginia since the royal government had collapsed almost a year earlier. Here Madison came into contact with some of Virginia's most prominent statesmen. On May 15, 1776, the convention voted, with Madison in the majority, to instruct its delegates to the Second Continental Congress to propose a declaration of independence.

A backbencher throughout all of his convention service, Madison's passionate belief in religious freedom informed his service on the committee to draft a declaration of rights and a new state constitution. George Mason, a prominent Fairfax County planter, drafted a declaration of rights which declared that "all men should enjoy the fullest Toleration in the Exercise of Religion, according to the Dictates of Conscience." At first, Madison attempted to win a complete disestablishment of the Anglican church. After this failed, he was able to replace Mason's draft with the positive statement that "all men are equally entitled to the free exercise of religion, according to the dictates of conscience."[20]

The Virginia convention adjourned on July 5, 1776, unaware that the Second Continental Congress had declared American independence. In October 1776 the convention reassembled. It was at this time that Madison met Thomas Jefferson. The two served on a committee on religion. Jefferson also advocated a complete separation of church and state. But like Madison's proposal, it was as yet too radical to be adopted.

In April 1777 Madison announced his intention to stand for election to the House of Delegates under the

20. Ibid., I, 175.

new state constitution of June 1776. The custom of the time called for candidates for public office to provide voters with "spirituous liquors, and other treats" on the election day—"swilling the planters with Bumpo" it was called. Madison was a righteous young man. He thought such practices "equally inconsistent with the purity of moral and of republican principles." His opponent, a tavern keeper, had no such qualms. The voters thought Madison was motivated by either "pride or parsimony." He lost the election,[21] but in the process he learned a valuable lesson. Madison returned to Montpelier out of public service; he never lost another election in his long political career.

On November 15, 1777, the House of Delegates elected Madison to the eight-man council of state, which shared executive power with the governor. His election to the council suggests that he was a well respected young politician. Madison's two years of service were momentous. Much of the day-to-day operation of government had been transferred from the occasionally sitting legislature to the council which sat daily except for the sickly season (mid–July to mid–November). The Continental Congress and the states faced desperate financial conditions as their paper money depreciated to worthlessness. Raising supplies to keep the army in the field became a struggle. As Madison took on more and more responsibility on the council, Governor Patrick Henry gave way to Benjamin Harrison and then to Thomas Jefferson. When the British army opened a new theater of action in the South, the situation became dangerous for Jefferson and Virginia.

Madison impressed Jefferson and the legislature with his hard work in one committee after another. His diligence was rewarded in December 1779, when the legislature elected Madison to represent Virginia in the

21. Madison to James K. Paulding, January 1832, ibid., I, 193.

Continental Congress. Madison informed Governor Harrison that he accepted the appointment and gave his "assurances that as far as fidelity and zeal can supply the place of abilities the interests of my Country shall be punctually promoted."[22] A difficult and arduous assignment for most, Madison eagerly embraced this new challenge.

IN CONGRESS, FOR THE FIRST TIME, 1781–1783

Madison had few of the hesitancies that other men had about going to Congress. Unmarried, he left no wife and children behind when he traveled to far-off Philadelphia. Because his father, in his late fifties, still managed the family plantation, Madison did not have to rely on an overseer and worry how the plantation (including the slaves) and other affairs were being handled. While many other delegates needed their salaries to meet their considerable expenses while in Philadelphia, Madison's family wealth provided him with financial security. Delegates from rural areas often found the urban life of Philadelphia unpleasant, but Madison looked forward to escaping from his "Obscure Corner" of the world and returning to "the Fountain-Head of Political and Literary Intelligence."[23] He had long looked forward to breathing the "free Air" of Philadelphia again—"it will mend my Constitution [that is his health] & confirm my principles."[24]

The work of Congress was primarily carried on in dozens of committees; the most active delegates had twenty to thirty committee assignments. Mornings and afternoons were spent either in formal congressional sessions or in committees, while in the evenings delegates often socialized in taverns, inns, and boarding houses

22. Williamsburg, December 16, 1779, ibid., I, 319.

23. Madison to William Bradford, Orange, April 28, 1783, ibid., I, 84.

24. Madison to William Bradford, Virginia, January 24, 1774, ibid., I, 106.

with fellow committee members, often discussing the difficult issues confronting their committees. Most members of Congress hated this committee drudgery as well as the monotony of Congress when it was actually in session. Madison reveled in it and wrote huge numbers of committee reports.

Seemingly Madison did not make a favorable first impression. He was always suspicious of "those impertinent fops that abound in every City to divert you from your business and philosophical amusements. You may please them more by admitting them to the enjoyment of your company but you will make them respect and admire you more be showing your indignation at their follies and by keeping them at a becoming distance." These fops, Madison felt, "breed in Towns and populous places, as naturally as flies do in the Shambles, because there they get food enough for their Vanity and impertinence."[25] Although almost thirty years old, Madison still looked like a teenager. Thomas Rodney of Delaware described his young colleague, "Who with some little reading in the Law is Just from the College, and possesses all the Self conceit that is Common to youth and inexperience in like cases—but is unattended with that gracefulness & ease which Sometimes Makes even the impertinence of youth and inexperience agreeable or at least not offensive."[26] Outside of Congress, Madison fared no better. Martha Dangerfield Bland, the wife of Congressman Theodorick Bland of Virginia, described the young congressman as "a gloomy, stiff creature. They say he is clever in Congress, but out of it, he has nothing

25. Madison to William Bradford, Orange, November 9, 1772, ibid., I, 75–76.

26. Thomas Rodney's Character Sketches of Some Members of Congress, post March 1781, Paul H. Smith, ed., *Letters of Delegates to Congress*, 1774–1789 (26 vols., Washington, D.C. 1976–2000), XVII, 36. Rodney was only seven years older than Madison, but Madison looked much younger.

engaging or even bearable in his Manners—the most unsociable creature in Existence."²⁷ This was perhaps the last time anyone would say unkind things about Madison's personality. He must have changed considerably during his Philadelphia years. In the future, even his political enemies would comment favorably on Madison's charm and social graces. As he left Philadelphia to return home in December 1783, Eliza House Trist, the daughter of the proprietor of Madison's boardinghouse, commented on Madison. "He has a Soul replete with gentleness, humanity and every social virtue." Surely, Trist felt, he could be elected governor of Virginia, but he "is too amiable in his disposition to bear up against a torrent of abuse. It will hurt his feelings and injure his health."²⁸

Madison left Virginia for Congress in March 1780 and did not return home at all until December 1783. Throughout this federal service, Madison advocated additional powers for Congress. During his first year, he led the movement to cede to Congress Virginia's claims to the land north and west of the Ohio River. He served on the Board of Admiralty and drafted Congress's instructions to U.S. minister to Spain, John Jay, calling on him to assert America's right to navigate the Mississippi River. Described as "a Young Gentleman of Industry and abilities," Madison was already considered one of the leading candidates for the new position of secretary for foreign affairs.²⁹

By his second year in Congress, Madison had established a reputation as a diligent, effective legislator—as a man who could write legislation and, through compromise, obtain consensus. In many respects he mirrored the

27. To Mrs. St. George Tucker, March 30, 1781, *Madison Papers*, II, 196n.

28. Eliza House Trist to Thomas Jefferson, April 13, 1784, Julian P. Boyd et al., eds. *The Papers of Thomas Jefferson* (Princeton, N.J., 1950–), VII, 97.

29. Thomas Burke to William Bingham, [Philadelphia, February 6?], 1781, Smith, *Letters of Delegates*, XVI, 682.

image of what George Washington thought a good, young legislator ought to be. "If you mean to be a respectable member, and to entitle yourself to the Ear of the House," speak "on important matters—and then make yourself thoroughly acquainted with the subject. Never be agitated by *more than* a decent *warmth*, & offer your sentiments with modest diffidence—opinions thus given, are listened to with more attention than when delivered in a dictatorial stile. The latter, if attended to at all, altho they may *force* conviction, is sure to convey disgust also."[30]

Madison was appointed to a three-man committee charged with drafting an amendment to the Articles of Confederation giving Congress coercive power over the states and their citizens. Madison premised the committee's report on the last of the articles, which provided "that every State shall abide by the determinations of the United States in Congress assembled on all questions which by this Confederation are submitted to them. And that the Articles of this Confederation shall be inviolably observed by every State." According to Madison, these provisions meant that Congress was vested with "a general and implied power . . . to enforce and carry into effect all the Articles of the said Confederation against any of the States which shall refuse or neglect to abide by such their determinations." Despite the specific limitation in Article II which provided that Congress had only those powers that were "expressly delegated" to it, Madison proposed to broaden the powers of Congress over the states and their citizens enormously. If the states failed to pay their requisitions, Congress could use the army and navy to force any delinquent states "to fulfill their federal

---

30. I'm indebted to Stuart Leiberger for making this comparison in his *Founding Friendship: George Washington, James Madison, and the Creation of the American Republic* (Charlottesville, Va., 1999), 82. Washington was actually addressing his nephew Bushrod Washington in a letter dated November 9, 1787.

engagements" by laying an embargo by land and sea on all trade between the delinquent state and other states and foreign countries. Congress's military forces could seize the ships and goods of any delinquent state or any citizen thereof. If Madison had his way, the whole federal relationship would be reversed. States would no longer retain their "sovereignty, freedom and independence." Congress would be supreme. Such a proposal was far too radical for most members of Congress. Consequently, Madison's report was referred to a grand committee (one member from each state), which proposed a far milder report, which was submitted to a series of small committees before being allowed to die without any final congressional action.[31]

During Madison's last year in Congress, he served on a committee that proposed a comprehensive financial program for the country. Largely melded together by Madison, the plan called for (1) a five percent impost on most imported goods for a maximum of twenty-five years earmarked exclusively to pay the interest and principal on the wartime debt, (2) an annual requisition of $1.5 million apportioned among the states, and (3) an encouragement of western land cessions to Congress by those states that had not yet ceded their western claims. In writing the address that accompanied the financial proposal to the states in April 1783, Madison argued that the success or failure of the Revolution and the future of republican forms of government depended upon how the states responded to the economic proposal.

The plan thus communicated and explained by Congress must now receive its fate from their

31. For Madison's proposed amendment, see Merrill Jensen, John P. Kaminski, and Gaspare J. Saladino, eds., *Constitutional Documents and Records, 1776–1787*, Volume I of *The Documentary History of the Ratification of the Constitution* (Madison, Wis., 1976), 141–43. Hereafter cited as DHRC.

Constituents. All the objects comprised in it are conceived to be of great importance to the happiness of this confederated republic, are necessary to render the fruits of the Revolution, a full reward for the blood, the toils, the cares and the calamities which have purchased it. . . . If justice, good faith, honor, gratitude & all the other Qualities which ennoble the character of a nation, and fulfill the ends of Government, be the fruits of our establishments, the cause of liberty will acquire a dignity and lustre, which it has never yet enjoyed; and an example will be set which can not but have the most favorable influence on the rights of mankind. If on the other side, our Governments should be unfortunately blotted with the reverse of these cardinal and essential Virtues, the great cause which we have engaged to vindicate, will be dishonored & betrayed; the last & fairest experiment in favor of the rights of human nature will be turned against them; and their patrons & friends exposed to be insulted & silenced by the votaries of Tyranny and Usurpation.[32]

Madison also played a key role in drafting an amendment to the Articles to apportion federal expenses based upon population. (For Madison's role in this amendment, see "Madison and Slavery," below.)

In June 1783, while Madison served in Congress, disgruntled soldiers from the Pennsylvania Line mutinied, descended on Philadelphia, surrounded the statehouse, and sent an ultimatum to the Pennsylvania Supreme Executive Council meeting in the statehouse demanding their back pay. Congress, which was also meeting in the statehouse, felt threatened and asked Pennsylvania

32. Address to the States, April 25–26, 1783, *Papers of James Madison*, VI, 492, 494.

President John Dickinson to call out the state militia. Dickinson refused. Congress adjourned to Princeton, where Madison spent his last days as a congressman. Madison grievously felt Congress's embarrassment at not being able to defend itself. Ashamed for his country, he realized how important it was for Congress to have coercive authority of its own territory and not to depend on any state for its protection.

Years later, Madison remembered some of the amusing aspects of Congress's exile in the tiny community of Princeton. Because of the lack of housing, Madison was forced to share a single small room with fellow Virginian Joseph Jones. The room had but one bed that the two congressmen shared. The bed so filled the room "that one was obliged to lie in bed while the other was dressing." It was a way, Madison joked, of "bringing members of Congress into close quarters."[33]

In December 1783, Madison, accompanied by Thomas Jefferson, briefly returned to Philadelphia and then traveled to Annapolis—yet another new residence for Congress. Just as Madison became the most prominent member of Congress, his federal career ended. The Articles of Confederation provided that congressional delegates could serve only three years in any six-year period. Madison had committed himself to the war effort and to acquiring increased power for Congress. He had become the most important member of Congress through his hard work in the federal cause. He was now forced to return to Montpelier and an uncertain future.

BACK IN VIRGINIA, 1784–1786

For the next three years Madison compartmentalized his life. Each year in the early fall he traveled north to New York and Philadelphia. Each spring, beginning in April

33. "CC" Proctor, ed., "After-Dinner Anecdotes of James Madison: Excerpts from Jared Sparks' Journal for 1829–31," *Virginia Magazine of History and Biography* 60 (1952), 264.

1784, Orange County electors sent him to the House of Delegates in Richmond. The last spring legislative session was held in 1784; thereafter the legislature met only once annually in October, usually adjourning sometime in January. When not traveling north or resident in Richmond, Madison resided at Montpelier.

Madison viewed Montpelier as both a haven and a prison. This was his home. As the eldest son he could be expected to take the lead in operating the plantation, but farming did not interest Madison at this time. His father and brothers recognized Madison's devotion to politics and government and seem willingly to have supported his career. But Madison's dependence on his family made him uncomfortable. Searching for an independent source of income for himself, he approached a number of people with land speculation schemes, but nothing materialized except a rather small venture with James Monroe along the Mohawk River in New York. Although Madison felt uneasy about it, he stayed resident on his father's plantation when not traveling north or in Richmond. Perhaps Madison's dependence on his father (his father lived until 1801, when Madison was fifty years old) had a psychological impact on why Madison wanted Congress to be financially independent of the states.

When at Montpelier Madison divided his time between family affairs and professional activities. He rose with the sun, busied himself with correspondence, and then had a light breakfast. Sequestered again, he read law; did research in his ever-growing library; prepared for the upcoming legislative session; read newspapers, political tracts, and scientific works. Madison's correspondence expanded with prominent Virginians at home, serving in Congress, and abroad. His favorite correspondent was Thomas Jefferson, his close friend serving as U.S. minister to France. Beginning in 1786, Madison's correspondence with George Washington increased significantly. Madison made time in the day for exercise. He walked and rode his horse around the estate. After dinner at 3 or 4:00, he spent time with the family and visitors talking about politics and business. Often the evenings ended playing Whist, a card game, for half bits until bedtime.

In the fall Madison usually traveled north. In September and October 1784 he participated in his most ambitious adventure. Linking up with the Marquis de Lafayette and French consul general Barbé–Marbois, they traveled to Fort Stanwix, the site of present-day Rome, N.Y., for a treaty conference with the Iroquois. Madison and his companions went deep into the wilderness, fording streams to visit the chief village of the Oneida. It was thrilling, but exhausting, and the trip bonded Madison and Lafayette for life. In 1785 and 1786 Madison again traveled north and spent time in Philadelphia and New York City, meeting with members of Congress and old friends in both cities. He also took the opportunity to buy books for his library.

In May and November of 1784, and October 1785 and 1786, Madison served in the Virginia House of Delegates. His remarkable service in Congress had created a reputation for excellent legislative work, and much was expected of him, though he had never served in the legislature. In mid–May 1784, William Short, soon to be Jefferson's private secretary in Paris, reported that "The Assembly have not yet proceeded to active Business. They have formed great Hopes of Mr. Madison, and those who know him best think he will not disappoint their most sanguine Expectations.[34] His close friend Edmund Randolph characterized him "as a general of whom much has been preconceived to his advantage."[35]

Madison did not disappoint. He quickly became one of several leaders in the House. He advocated an agenda

34. Short to Thomas Jefferson, Richmond, May 15, 1784, *Papers of Thomas Jefferson*, VII, 260.

35. Randolph to Thomas Jefferson, Richmond, May 15, 1784, ibid., 257.

of reform, economic recovery, and stabilization at home and nationally, increased powers for Congress, and a defense of the rights of individuals. In particular, Madison hoped to enact the revised code of laws drafted by Thomas Jefferson, George Wythe, and Edmund Pendleton in 1777–79. To ensure success, Madison sought the support of Patrick Henry, but soon it was obvious that Henry would oppose everything that Madison favored. Henry's election as governor removed his powerful personality and oratory from the floor of the House, but Henry's opposition from outside was still a mighty force for Madison to overcome. Nevertheless, over the course of three years, Madison succeeded in getting over 40 of the remaining 117 revised laws enacted. Archibald Stuart, one of Madison's legislative allies, praised his efforts. "Can you suppose it possible that Madison should shine with more than usual splendor [in] this Assembly. It is sir not only possible but a fact. He has astonished mankind & has by means perfectly constitutional become almost a Dictator upon all subjects, that the House have not so far prejudged as to shut their Ears from Reason & armed their minds from Conviction. His influence alone has hitherto overcome the impatience of the house & carried them half thro the Revised Code."[36] Madison failed, however, to enact two of the most important reforms—an act establishing a public school system and an act revising the state's penal code. Madison was also unsuccessful at getting a reform of the state's judiciary and a revision of the state constitution. Jefferson could only console Madison from Europe by saying "What we have to do I think is devoutly to pray for [Henry's] death."[37]

Probably the most important action of the legislature during Madison's three-year tenure was the enactment of Jefferson's bill for religious freedom. In 1784 Patrick

36. Stuart to John Breckinridge, Richmond, December 7, 1785, *Papers of James Madison*, VIII, 446.

37. Jefferson to Madison, Paris, December 8, 1784, ibid., VIII, 178.

Henry, Richard Henry Lee, and Edmund Pendleton introduced legislation to allow public funds to be used to support Christian ministers. Through a series of adroit delaying tactics and his anonymously written Memorial and Remonstrances against Religious Assessments, Madison was able not only to kill the general assessment act, but in January 1786 to win approval for Jefferson's bill. Madison wrote Jefferson that they had "extinguished for ever the ambitious hope of making laws for the human mind."[38]

MADISON AND SLAVERY

James Madison, like many other Southern leaders of the Revolutionary era, abhorred the institution of slavery. In time, it was expected that slavery would wither and die. But in the meantime, in the Southern culture, slavery was looked upon as the norm. Slaves were necessary in the Southern economy and to serve their masters. Madison was born and raised in this kind of a society. When Madison was only eight years old, his grandmother deeded him in trust an infant slave to be raised alongside Master Jemmy. Billey and Jemmy were raised almost as brothers. But then, at a certain age, both of them realized that there was a difference: one was black, the other white; one was a slave, the other master.

To complicate matters further, the Revolutionary rhetoric preached the doctrine of liberty and freedom while denouncing the new British imperial policy that, if left unchecked, would enslave Americans. Both white and black Americans saw the incongruity of Patriots struggling for their freedom from potential enslavement while keeping a whole race of men, women, and children in bondage. Slave owners' self-interest vied with their philosophical antipathy for slavery, while the specter of slave

38. Richmond, January 22, 1786, ibid., VIII, 474.

insurrections always haunted Southern planters.

While serving in Congress in 1783, Madison participated in the debate over how to apportion federal expenses among the states. The provision in the Articles of
Confederation basing the requisition of federal taxes
among the states on the value of land simply did not work.
Most states did not submit their estimated valuations of
lands and those states that did submit valuations, naturally undervalued their land. Congress agreed that an
amendment to the Articles of Confederation should
apportion federal expenses among the states based upon
population. The debate ultimately focused on whether or
not to count slaves as part of the population for apportioning the taxes. Delegates from Northern states argued
that slaves, as people, should be counted; Southern delegates, however, argued that slaves were property and
therefore should not be counted. Various delegates suggested compromises. Madison proposed that three-fifths
of the slaves be counted in apportioning federal taxes.
Congress accepted Madison's proposal and thus was
established "the federal ratio." Although not officially
adopted by all the state legislatures, the population
amendment with the three-fifths clause was used by the
Confederation Congress in the requisitions of 1786 and
1787,[39] and was adopted by the Federal Convention of 1787
as the ratio for counting slaves both for purposes of representation and direct taxation—the infamous three-fifths
clause of the Constitution.

When Madison finished his congressional service, he
wrote to his father that he would be home soon, but that
Billey would not return with him. "On a view of all cir-

39. Congressional debates, March 6 to April 18, 1783, John P.
Kaminski, ed., *A Necessary Evil? Slavery and the Debate Over the
Constitution* (Madison, Wis., 1995), 20–23. Madison's three-fifths pro-
posal was made on March 28 (p. 22). Eleven states adopted the popu-
lation amendment of April 18, 1783. Only New Hampshire and Rhode
Island did not adopt it.

cumstances I have judged it most prudent not to force Billey back to Virginia even if [it] could be done." Billey's mind, according to Madison, was "too thoroughly tainted to be a fit companion for fellow slaves in Virginia." Madison did not blame Billey "for coveting that liberty for which we have paid the price of so much blood, and have proclaimed so often to be the right, & worthy the pursuit, of every human being." Instead of freeing Billey, Madison sold him into indentured servitude for seven years—the maximum allowable time under Pennsylvania law. He knew that he would not "get near the worth of him" from the transaction,[40] but this was a way for Billey to learn a trade that could sustain him as a free man.

Out of national politics, Madison continued reading law. He did not, however, wish to make the law his full-time profession. But, he wrote, "Another of my wishes is to depend as little as possible on the labour of slaves."[41] In the Virginia House of Delegates, Madison observed the hostile response to the Methodist ministers' petition campaign to abolish slavery. "The pulse of the House of Delegates was felt on Thursday with regard to a general manumission by a petition presented on that subject. It was rejected without dissent. . . . A motion was made to throw it under the table"—a sign of contempt. Counter petitions were offered opposing "any step towards freeing the slaves, and even praying for a repeal of the law which" made manumissions by individuals easier.[42] Slavery could not be abolished by law nor in the immediate future.

When Madison acknowledged that the great division in the Federal Convention was not between large and small states but "between the Northern & Southern" states—he meant those states "having or not having

40. James Madison to James Madison, Sr., Philadelphia, September 8, 1783, ibid., 268.

41. Madison to Edmund Randolph, Orange, Va., July 26, 1785, ibid.

42. James Madison to George Washington, Richmond, November 11, 1785, ibid., 36.

slaves." Feeling strongly that the interests of both the slave states and non-slave states needed to be protected, he suggested that instead of using the "federal ratio" of three-fifths of the slaves in computing representation in both houses of Congress, that one house be apportioned "according to the number of free inhabitants only; and in the other according to the whole number counting the slaves as if free. By this arrangement the Southern Scale would have the advantage in one House, and the Northern in the other." Madison felt uneasy about making such a proposal because of "his unwillingness to urge any diversity of interests on an occasion when it is but too apt to arise of itself" and because of "the inequality of powers that must be vested in the two branches, and which would destroy the equilibrium of interests."[43] Madison's proposal never received serious consideration.

Madison and most of his fellow Convention delegates wanted an immediate close of the African slave trade. He and George Mason strenuously spoke out against the provision that would prohibit Congress from closing the African trade before 1808. "Twenty years," Madison pleaded, "will produce all the mischief that can be apprehended from the liberty to import slaves. So long a term will be more dishonorable to the American character than to say nothing about it in the Constitution."[44] Madison also strove to keep any mention of the word *slavery* out of the Constitution, thinking "it wrong to admit . . . the idea that there could be property in men."[45]

One of the most important actions of the first federal Congress under the Constitution was to provide a revenue for the new government, most of which was expected to come from a five-percent tariff on imports. Toward the end of the debate over the tariff in May 1789, Madison had a proposal introduced to levy a $10 tax on

43. Madison Speech of June 30, 1787, ibid., 47.
44. Madison Speech of August 25, 1787, ibid., 62–63.
45. Ibid., 64.

every slave brought into America—the maximum tax allowed under Article I, section 9 of the Constitution. Madison supported the duty from "the dictates of humanity, the principles of the people, the national safety and happiness, and prudent policy." "It is hoped," he said, "that by expressing a national disapprobation of this trade, we may destroy it, and save ourselves from reproaches, and our posterity the imbecility ever attendant on a country filled with slaves." In a rare statement in support of a broad interpretation of the Constitution and a reference to the danger of slave insurrections that the federal government might have to suppress, Madison suggested that "It is a necessary duty of the general government to protect every part of the empire against danger, as well internal as external; every thing therefore which tends to encrease this danger, though it may be a local affair, yet if it involves national expence or safety, becomes of concern to every part of the union, and is a proper subject for the consideration of those charged with the general administration of the government."[46] After a vehement debate over the tax on imported slaves that threatened the entire tariff bill, Madison agreed to withdraw his proposal to be resubmitted as a separate bill later in the session. Such a bill was proposed in September 1789 but postponed until the next session. No further consideration of a tax on imported slaves occurred until 1804 when South Carolina reopened its foreign slave trade.

In response to petitions from the abolition societies of Pennsylvania and New York and from Quakers from Pennsylvania to Virginia, the U.S. House of Representatives debated whether Congress could (1) immediately prohibit the African slave trade, (2) reg-

46. Madison Speech in the U.S. House of Representatives, May 13, 1789, ibid., 207–9. This was dangerously close to the interpretation of the Constitution that Patrick Henry had made in the Virginia ratifying convention in warning about the possibility of a federal abolition of slavery.

ulate the African slave trade, (3) emancipate slaves throughout the United States, and/or (4) regulate the condition of slaves throughout the country. The debate was vehement and continued from late February through late March 1790. The petitions were referred to a committee chaired by Madison which concluded that Congress could not prohibit the African slave trade before 1808 (as specified in Article V) and could not abolish or interfere with the institution of slavery where it existed. Congress could, however, regulate the African slave trade under its power to regulate commerce. Madison wanted these conclusions to be entered on the House journals "for the information of the public." Such a public statement would show that Congress would act whenever it could constitutionally. It would also satisfy those Southern representatives who had been so ardent in the debate, and it would "tend to quiet the apprehensions of the Southern states, by recognizing that Congress had no power whatever to prohibit the importation of slaves prior to the year 1808, or to manumit them at any time."[47]

In June 1791 Robert Pleasants, a prominent Quaker merchant from Henrico County, Va., asked Madison to submit a memorial to Congress from the Virginia Abolition Society that condemned slavery and asked for an amelioration of the conditions of the African slave trade. Pleasants also asked Madison to submit a petition to the Virginia legislature calling for the gradual abolition of slavery in the state that would end "an Evil of great Magnitude." Living "in an enlightened age, when liberty is allowed to be the unalienable right of all mankind," Pleasants felt that "it surely behooves us of the present generation, and more especially the Legislature, to endeavour to restore one of the most valuable blessings of life, to an injured and unhappy race of people."[48]

47. Madison Speech in the U.S. House of Representatives, March 23, 1790, ibid., 229.

48. Pleasants to Madison, June 6, 1791, ibid., 270.

Madison turned down both requests. He replied that his constituents were "greatly interested in that species of property," and "it would seem that I might be chargeable at least with want of candour, if not of fidelity, were I to make use of a situation in which their confidence has placed me, to become a volunteer in giving a public wound, as they would deem it, to an interest on which they set so great a value." Madison also believed that the Quaker memorial would have little chance of success in Congress no matter who introduced it. In fact, though Madison in 1790 had argued that Congress could regulate the foreign slave trade, Congress never enacted any regulations to ameliorate the atrocious conditions under which slaves were transported from Africa to America.

Madison felt that the petition to the Virginia legislature seeking a gradual abolition of slavery was a matter "of great delicacy and importance." The consequences of such a petition "ought to be weighed by those who would hazard it." In all likelihood, Madison wrote, the petition would "do harm rather than good." Perhaps the legislature would make it more difficult to manumit slaves and might even restore the old law requiring freedmen to leave the state within a year of their manumission.[49]

Madison, like his close friend Thomas Jefferson, denounced slavery but believed that blacks were inherently inferior to whites. This racism deepened as Madison grew older and profoundly affected his attitude toward emancipation. Abolition of slavery could take place only in a three-step process: (1) a gradual system of emancipation with public compensation for slave owners had to be accompanied by (2) the colonization of free blacks apart from white society, and (3) the introduction of an alternative work force to replace the freed slaves.[50] Madison did

49. Madison to Pleasants, Philadelphia, October 30, 1791, ibid., 271–72.

50. See Madison's Memorandum on an African Colony for Freed Slaves, c. October 20, 1789, ibid., 269.

little to implement this difficult process. When asked to lead, he declined; and as years passed, he despaired that much could be done to rid the country of this terrible injustice. Madison and his Southern brethren were willing to risk their all for their own independence; they refused to take similar risks for the liberty of enslaved blacks.

CHANGING THE CONSTITUTION

A decade after declaring their independence, most Americans felt dissatisfied with their governments—both state and federal. Infused with the optimism of the Enlightenment philosophy and with a sense of mission for all of mankind, Americans had confidently crafted state and federal constitutions between 1776 and 1780. When these written constitutions failed to answer all their needs, Americans worried that the Revolutionary principles they had fought so hard to preserve might be lost as republican governments succumbed to one form or another of despotic rule. The Federal Convention of 1787 seemed to offer the last hope that the people could actually determine their own forms of government through reflection and choice rather than tamely submitting to governments imposed by force or chance.

Throughout his tenure in the Virginia House of Delegates, Madison had sought to strengthen the powers of Congress. He hoped that Virginia would lead the way, and, during the October 1785 session, he worked to have the legislature adopt an amendment to the Articles of Confederation that would give Congress the power to regulate commerce. When that effort failed, a motion was introduced by John Tyler to call a general convention of the states to address commercial concerns.[51] After delaying consideration for almost two months, the House and

51. Historians have debated whether Madison was the driving force behind this motion for a commercial convention, using Tyler only to keep Madison's opponents from staunchly opposing the proposal.

Senate overwhelmingly adopted the measure on January 21, 1786, the last day of the session. Madison had previously opposed such unorthodox methods, preferring to work within the legislature and Congress. Now, however, Madison felt that though it would "probably miscarry," a commercial convention was "better than nothing, and . . . may possibly lead to better consequences than at first occur."[52]

The legislature appointed Madison and seven other commissioners to attend the convention—a delegation so large that Madison feared it might "stifle the thing in its birth."[53] The convention was "to consider how far a uniform system" of "commercial regulations may be necessary" for the "common interest and . . . permanent harmony" of the country. The Virginia commissioners decided to hold the convention in September 1786 in Annapolis, Maryland. Madison explained that "It was thought prudent to avoid the neighbourhood of Congress [i.e., New York City], and the large Commercial towns [i.e., Philadelphia], in order to disarm the adversaries to the object, of insinuations of influence from either of these quarters."[54] Madison worried that if the convention failed, it would confirm "Great Britain and all the world in the belief that we are not to be respected, nor apprehended as a nation in matters of Commerce."[55] Although he was pessimistic about the convention's success, "Yet on the whole," Madison wrote, " I cannot disapprove of the experiment. Something it is agreed is necessary to be done, towards the commerce at least of the U.S., and if anything can be done, it seems as likely to result from the

52. Madison to James Monroe, Richmond, January 22, 1786, *Papers of James Madison*, VIII, 483.

53. Ibid., VIII, 483.

54. Madison to Thomas Jefferson, Orange, March 18, 1786, ibid., VIII, 501–2.

55. Ibid., 502.

proposed Convention, and more likely to result from the present crisis, than from any other mode or time. If nothing can be done we may at least expect a full discovery as to that matter from the experiment, and such a piece of knowledge will be worth the trouble and expence of obtaining it."[56]

Nine states elected commissioners to the convention, including Madison and Alexander Hamilton of New York. Before the September meeting, Madison and others got the idea that the convention might be used as a springboard to a more ambitious convention. Madison confided to Jefferson in mid–August that "Gentlemen both within & without Congress wish to make this Meeting subservient to a plenipotentiary Convention for amending the Confederation."[57] Some people, particularly in New England, suspected as much. Boston merchant Stephen Higginson wrote that "political" not "commercial" objects were being sought. The men elected as commissioners were all "esteemed great aristocrats . . . few of them have been in the commercial line, nor is it probable they know or care much about commercial objects."[58]

Twelve commissioners from five states met in Annapolis on September 11. Without waiting for others to arrive, the delegates hastily wrote a report and adjourned. The convention called for a general convention of the states to meet in Philadelphia in May 1787 "to devise such further provisions as shall appear to them necessary to render the constitution of the Federal Government adequate to the exigencies of the Union." Madison was delighted. He determined to assure that Virginia would elect the best possible delegation to this new convention.

Before the Annapolis convention assembled, Shays's Rebellion broke out in Massachusetts. Violence or dis-

56. Madison to James Monroe, Orange, March 14, 1786, ibid., VIII, 498.

57. Madison to Jefferson, August 12, 1786, ibid., IX, 96.

58. Quoted in *Constitutional Documents and Records*, 177.

turbances of one kind or another occurred in a half dozen other states as well. In Virginia two county courthouses were burned to the ground, conveniently destroying all of the tax records. Anxiety filled the country. A crisis loomed. George Washington wrote that "There are combustibles in every State, which a spark might set fire to."[59]

Madison also felt the urgency. With a sense of foreboding, he worked feverishly hard to prepare himself for the upcoming convention. He turned down diplomatic appointments to The Netherlands and Spain, partly because of his fear of ocean travel and partly because he sensed that America was the place for him to be. Between April and June 1786 Madison read widely from his library at Montpelier on ancient and modern confederations. As a man of the Enlightenment, he believed in the utility of history, and Madison hoped to discover the weaknesses of confederacies and how to guard against these fatal flaws. He convinced himself that confederacies were fragile and that they tended either to dissolve or become impotent when they lacked a central controlling power. Because the Annapolis convention adjourned so quickly, Madison never was able to use his findings in that convention's debates. He would further develop his ideas about confederations for use in the next Convention and in the public debate that would follow.

The Virginia legislature considered the Annapolis report in November, and on the 23rd passed an act authorizing the election of seven delegates to the Federal Convention to meet in Philadelphia in May. Madison wrote the authorizing act—a powerful piece of political propaganda that was sent to all of the state governors and legislatures encouraging them to appoint delegates to the Convention. Madison's act, like the Declaration of

59. Washington to Henry Knox, Mount Vernon, December 26, 1786, W. W. Abbot, ed., *The Papers of George Washington, Confederation Series* (Charlottesville, Va.), IV, 482.

Independence a decade earlier, stated the "necessity" of America's situation. No one could

> doubt that the crisis is arrived at which the good people of America are to decide the solemn question, whether they will by wise and magnanimous efforts reap the just fruits of that Independence, which they have so gloriously acquired, and of that Union which they have cemented with so much of their common blood; or whether by giving way to unmanly jealousies and prejudices, or to partial and transitory interests, they will renounce the auspicious blessings prepared for them by the Revolution, and furnish to its enemies an eventual triumph over those by whose virtue and valour it has been accomplished.

Changes were necessary that would "render the United States as happy in peace as they have been glorious in war."[60]

On December 4, 1786, the legislature elected Madison, George Washington, Patrick Henry, Edmund Randolph, George Mason, George Wythe, and John Blair as delegates to the upcoming Convention. Even without Henry, who refused the appointment, it was the most prestigious of the state delegations. Washington was by far the most important delegate from any state, and without the ongoing pressure from Madison and Randolph, he would not have attended the Convention. Madison told Washington "the advantage of having your name in the front of the appointment as a mark of the earnestness of Virginia, and an invitation to the most select characters from every part of the Confederacy, ought at all events to be made use of."[61] On the day the

---

60. *Constitutional Documents and Records*, 197.

61. Madison to Washington, Richmond, December 7, 1786, ibid. IX, 199.

delegation was elected, Madison wrote to Jefferson that there had been a "revolution of sentiment which the experience of one year has affected in this Country."[62] The time was ripe to make a serious change in the Articles of Confederation.

IN CONGRESS, A SECOND TIME

On November 7, 1786, the Virginia legislature elected Madison to return to Congress. His three-year "exile" from national politics was over. Madison returned to Montpelier from Richmond on January 11 and four days later left for New York City. David Stuart, a legislative colleague, wrote Washington that "I have no doubt Mr. Madison's virtues and abilities make it necessary that he should be in Congress, but from what I already foresee, I shall dread the consequences of another Assembly without him."[63]

Madison attended Congress on February 10, 1787, and immediately resumed his position of leadership. With Shays's Rebellion suppressed, Charles Pinckney of South Carolina moved that Congress suspend the enlistment of troops authorized in October to combat "Indian uprisings" on the frontier. Madison, without addressing the propriety or constitutionality of raising an army to suppress an internal insurrection within a state, strongly opposed Pinckney's motion because he was uncertain "that the spirit of insurrection was subdued" and because the mobilization of troops by Lord Dorchester in Canada might allow the British "to take advantage of events in this Country."[64] Madison also endorsed a report by Secretary for Foreign Affairs John Jay that condemned

62. Madison to Jefferson, Richmond, December 4, 1786, *Papers of James Madison*, IX, 189.

63. Stuart to Washington, Richmond, December 25, 1786, *Washington Papers, Confederation Series*, IV, 477.

64. James Madison, Notes of Debates, February 19, 1787, *Papers of James Madison*, IX, 278.

the states' repeated violations of the Treaty of Peace and unequivocally proclaimed Congress's "exclusive right and power" over foreign affairs.[65] Finally, Madison joined other Southerners in condemning Congress's alteration of its instructions to Secretary Jay that would allow him, if necessary, to cede the American right to navigate the Mississippi River in exchange for a commercial treaty with Spain. The intense debate over this sectionally divisive issue convinced everyone that such a cession would never be allowed; it also shook the unity of those who espoused giving more power to the federal government. Sectionalism was now an additional factor endangering the Confederation.

PREPARING FOR THE CONVENTION

Madison continued to prepare himself and his state's delegation for the Philadelphia Convention. He wrote a memorandum on the "Vices of the Political System of the United States" and drafted the outline of a new constitution that would replace—not simply revise—the Articles of Confederation. Drawing upon theory and America's experience since 1776, Madison demonstrated the weaknesses of the Articles and the "multiplicity," "mutability," and "injustice" of state laws—innumerable laws that were often repealed by subsequent legislatures and that sometimes violated the rights of individuals. He acknowledged and endorsed the basic feature of republican government—that the majority should rule—but denounced the tendency of majorities to tyrannize over minorities. Without a coercive authority, Congress under the Articles of Confederation could not collect taxes, regulate commerce, enforce treaties, defend states against internal insurrections, or prevent states from encroaching on Congress's power, trespassing on the rights of other states, or violating the liberties of their citizens. According to

65. *Journals of Congress*, XXXII, 177–84.

Madison, these "vices" required a fundamental alteration in the country's constitution.

Madison outlined his plan for a new constitution in a remarkable series of letters to George Washington, Edmund Randolph, Thomas Jefferson, and Edmund Pendleton from February through April 1787. As the convention neared, he felt the pressure mount. Somehow Madison believed that the responsibility for success or failure rested on his shoulders. Virginia would be expected to take the lead and he would have to be the driving force on the Virginia delegation. The Convention was perhaps America's last chance freely and rationally to choose its government. Madison was convinced that "unless the Union be organized efficiently & on Republican Principles, innovations of a much more objectionable form may be obtruded [i.e., monarchy or aristocracy], or in the most favorable event, the partition of the Empire into rival & hostile confederacies will ensue."[66] He wrote his friend and mentor Edmund Pendleton that "The nearer the crisis approaches, the more I tremble for the issue. The necessity of gaining the concurrence of the Convention in some system that will answer the purpose, the subsequent approbation of Congress, and the final sanction of the States, presents a series of chances, which would inspire despair in any case where the alternative was less formidable." What made matters particularly difficult was the necessity of augmenting Congress's power and reducing the power of the states and then getting the state legislatures and the people to agree to such monumental changes.[67]

Madison's letter to his close friend, Governor Edmund Randolph, is particularly revealing. As delicately as he could, Madison disagreed with Randolph's plan to revise the Articles of Confederation by jettisoning the bad

66. Madison to Edmund Randolph, New York, April 8, 1787, *Papers of James Madison*, IX, 371.

67. Madison to Pendleton, New York, April 22, 1787, ibid., IX, 395.

provisions and adding new ones in their place. Madison preferred a completely new constitution and incorporating only "the valuable articles into the new System." "An explanatory address" should accompany the new constitution when it was sent to the people, who would have to accept or reject the whole new system. Adoption of only some provisions would be unacceptable.[68]

As a fundamental belief Madison felt that the American Union—"the idea of an aggregate sovereignty"—could not survive if the states retained their "sovereignty, freedom and independence" as provided in Article II of the Articles of Confederation. At the same time Madison realized that consolidating the states "into one simple republic" was not only "unattainable," but also "inexpedient." A "middle ground" had to be found "which will at once support a due supremacy of the national authority, and leave in force the local authorities so far as they can be subordinately useful."

The first principle that had to be changed was representation. The unicameral Confederation Congress, where each state had one vote regardless of population or wealth, had to give way to a bicameral Congress in which representation in both houses was apportioned according to population or by contributions (payment of taxes). The large states had accepted equal state voting under the Confederation because Congress had no authority over individuals—it could only act upon states—and Congress had no coercive power to enforce acts that the large states disliked and chose to violate. But under a government that acted directly on the people as individuals, "the case would be materially altered." The states would have to be fairly represented in Congress.

The national government would have to "be armed with a positive & complete authority in all cases where uniform measures are necessary." This meant that

68. Madison to Randolph, New York, April 8, 1787, ibid., IX, 369.

Congress should retain all the powers that it had under the Confederation but also be given the power to regulate commerce, to levy and collect taxes, to raise an army and navy, etc. Congress must also have the power (as the king in council had before the Revolution) to veto "in all cases whatsoever" any and all acts passed by the state legislatures. In an extraordinary statement, Madison said that he conceived this power "to be essential and the least possible abridgement of the State Sovereignties. Without such a defensive power, every positive power that can be given on paper will be unavailing." He also believed that this kind of congressional control over state legislation would "give internal stability to the States" and protect the rights of people.

A federal judiciary would also have to be created to which people could ultimately appeal. "If the judges in the last resort depend on the States & are bound by their oaths to them and not to the Union, the intention of the law and the interests of the nation may be defeated by the obsequiousness of the Tribunals to the policy or prejudices of the States. It seems at least essential that an appeal should lie to some national tribunals in all cases which concern foreigners, or inhabitants of other States."

Congress, Madison argued, should have two houses. One should be elected directly by the people or by the state legislatures for a short term. A second, smaller chamber with a longer term should be elected by a different constituency and might have staggered terms. This chamber might have the veto power over state legislation.

Madison also called for a separate, single executive. He was unclear about exactly what powers this officer would have, but he thought it might, in combination with some federal judges, form a council of revision, which would serve, in essence, as a third branch of the legislature. Every bill passed by Congress would need the approval of this council. This would be a far more effective method of bringing the authority and experience of judges into legislation than judicial review. New York had such a council in its 1777 constitution, and Madison seemed to think it functioned well. The legislature could override council vetoes by a two-thirds vote of both houses.

The new constitution should "expressly guarantee the tranquility of the States against internal as well as external dangers." To give this new constitution "proper energy," it should be adopted "by the authority of the people, and not merely by that of the [state] Legislatures."

Madison realized that these might seem to be "extravagant" and "unattainable" proposals, and thus "unworthy of being attempted." But he believed that they went "no further than is essential" and that at this time of crisis, they were attainable.

THE CONSTITUTIONAL CONVENTION

Madison left Congress in New York City on May 2 and arrived in Philadelphia three days later before any non-Pennsylvania delegate had arrived and three weeks before the Convention formed a quorum. His fellow Virginia delegates also arrived early and for a week they caucused "two or three hours every day, in order to form a proper correspondence of sentiments."[69] The Virginia Plan, primarily a compilation of Madison's ideas, was agreed upon, and Governor Randolph—an eloquent speaker—was selected to present the plan at the outset of the Convention. Randolph presented Virginia's proposal on May 29, the first day of debate. It stunned everyone as a revolution in government. On June 16, supporters of minimal amendments to the Articles presented their plan. Then, in what was either a brilliant piece of strategy or a completely fortuitous event, Alexander Hamilton on June 18 presented an even more radical proposal than Virginia's

69. George Mason to George Mason, Jr., Philadelphia, May 20, 1787, Max Farrand, ed., *The Records of the Federal Convention of 1787* (3 vols., New Haven, Conn., 1911), III, 23.

outlining a strong national government that some saw as veering toward monarchy. Suddenly the Virginia Plan did not look so radical—in fact it was now the centrist plan. The Convention voted on June 19 to reject the plan to amend the Articles and to continue with the Virginia Plan as the basis for debate.

Madison had three primary goals in the Convention: (1) he wanted to replace the weak confederation government that acted upon strong sovereign states with a powerful national government that could act directly on individuals and was dominant over the states; (2) he wanted to replace the equal representation of the states in a unicameral congress with a bicameral congress in which the states were represented proportionally; and (3) he wanted the central government to have a veto power over the legislation of the states "in all cases whatsoever." He succeeded in his first goal, but only partially in accomplishing the second and third.

While in the Convention Madison spoke over 200 times. Only Gouverneur Morris and James Wilson (both representing Pennsylvania) exceeded him. He spoke authoritatively on every subject. His knowledge was unsurpassed. The position espoused by Madison was usually adopted by the Convention. Fellow Convention delegate William Pierce of Georgia explained how this timid, young Virginian came to have such an impact. Madison

> is a character who has long been in public life; and what is very remarkable every Person seems to acknowledge his greatness. He blends together the profound politician with the Scholar. In the management of every great question he evidently took the lead in the Convention, and tho' he cannot be called an Orator, he is a most agreeable, eloquent, and convincing Speaker. From a spirit of industry and application which he possesses in

a most eminent degree, he always comes forward the best informed Man on any point in debate. The affairs of the United States, he perhaps, has the most correct knowledge of, of any Man in the Union. He has been twice a Member of Congress, and was always thought one of the ablest Members that ever sat in that Council. Mr. Maddison is about 37 years of age, a Gentleman of great modesty,—with a remarkable sweet temper. He is easy and unreserved among his acquaintance, and has a most agreeable style of conversation.[70]

Echoing Pierce, Thomas Jefferson wrote in his autobiography that Madison had "at ready command the rich resources of his luminous and discriminating mind." Madison's "extensive information rendered him the first of every assembly of which he became a member."[71]

Toward the end of the Convention, Madison served on the five-man Committee of Style that wrote the final language of the Constitution. Although he signed the Constitution (with the tiniest cribbed signature of the thirty-nine signers), Madison was sorely disappointed in the final product. Actually, he believed that he had failed. During the four months the Convention sat, Madison and Jefferson continued their long-time correspondence. While the Convention was in session, Madison could not divulge to his friend the details of the proceedings, which was forbidden by the secrecy rule. But Madison assured Jefferson that "as soon as I am at liberty I will endeavor to make amends for my silence."[72] Madison predicted that "there can be no doubt but that the result [of the

70. Farrand, III, 94–95.

71. Merrill D. Peterson, ed., *Thomas Jefferson: Writings* (New York, 1984), 37.

72. Madison to Jefferson, Philadelphia, July 18, 1787, *Papers of James Madison*, X, 105.

Convention] will in some way or other have a powerful effect on our destiny."[73] Shortly before the Convention adjourned, Madison confided to Jefferson his disappointment in how things turned out. He feared that the proposed constitution "will neither effectually answer its national object nor prevent the local mischiefs which every where excite disgusts against the state governments."[74] It took six weeks for the dejected Madison to explain to his friend the difficulties faced by the Convention and how the lack of a congressional veto over state laws would seriously weaken the central government.

One of Madison's most important contributions at the Convention was his note-taking. While doing research on ancient and modern confederations a year earlier, Madison was disappointed in finding "very imperfect account[s], of their structure, and of the attributes and functions of the presiding Authority." His "curiosity" was not satisfied "especially in what related to the process, the principles, the reasons, & the anticipations, which prevailed in the formation of them." He thus determined "to preserve as far as I could an exact account of what might pass in the Convention," knowing how grateful future generations would be. He also realized how valuable such a record would be for historians in studying "a Constitution on which would be staked the happiness of a people great even in its infancy, and possibly the cause of Liberty throughout the world." Sometime during the early 1830s, in an essay obviously meant as an introduction to a printed edition of his Convention notes, Madison described the procedure he used for taking notes.

> In pursuance of the task I had assumed I chose a
> seat in front of the presiding member, with the

73. Madison to Jefferson, Philadelphia, June 6, 1787, ibid., X, 29.
74. Madison to Jefferson, Philadelphia, September 6, 1787, ibid., X, 163–64.

other members, on my right & left hands. In this favorable position for hearing all that passed, I noted in terms legible & in abbreviations & marks intelligible to myself what was read from the Chair or spoken by the members; and losing not a moment unnecessarily between the adjournment & reassembling of the Convention I was enabled to write out my daily notes during the session or within a few finishing days after its close in the extent and form preserved in my own hand on my files. . . . It happened, also, that I was not absent a single day, nor more than a casual fraction of an hour in any day, so that I could not have lost a single speech, unless a very short one.[75]

Madison's experience at taking notes of the debates in Congress during the early 1780s and in the first half of 1787 assisted him in note-taking in the Convention.

Although over the years Madison received many requests for information about his notes, he almost always refused access to them except for a very few people, among whom was Thomas Jefferson. When asked for information about what the Federal Convention did, Madison referred inquirers to the printed debates from the state ratifying conventions and the public debate in newspapers, broadsides, and pamphlets. Not until 1840— four years after his death—were his papers published in a three-volume edition. Two of the three volumes contained his Convention notes. They remain today the most thorough and reliable record of what transpired in the Federal Convention—a precious gift from Madison to his country.

75. Adrienne Koch, ed., *Notes of Debates in the Federal Convention of 1787 Reported by James Madison* (New York, 1966, reprint edition, 1987), 17–18.

RATIFYING THE CONSTITUTION

Despite his disappointment with the Constitution, Madison praised the work of the Convention and the Constitution itself. In an extraordinary statement by a man who believed in the complete separation of church and state, Madison wrote that the Constitution was divinely inspired. With all the difficulties in drafting a constitution for such a diverse country,

> The real wonder is, that so many difficulties should have been surmounted; and surmounted with a unanimity almost as unprecedented as it must have been unexpected. It is impossible for any man of candor to reflect on this circumstance, without partaking of the astonishment. It is impossible for the man of pious reflection not to perceive in it, a finger of that Almighty hand which has been so frequently and signally extended to our relief in the critical stages of the revolution.[76]

Madison even praised the fact that the Convention had created a Constitution different from his original conception. He wrote that it was "wonderful" that the Convention was "forced into some deviations from the artificial structure and regular symmetry, which an abstract view of the subject might lead an ingenious theorist to bestow on a Constitution planned in his closet or in his imagination."[77]

Madison left Philadelphia on September 21 to return to Congress in New York City. On September 26–28 he participated in the debate over sending the Constitution to the states for their consideration. Federalists (supporters of the Constitution) in Congress (27 of the 32 dele-

76. *The Federalist* 37, New York *Daily Advertiser*, January 11, 1788, DHRC, XV, 348.

77. Ibid.

gates present) wanted to send the Constitution to the states with the endorsement of Congress. Antifederalists (opponents of the Constitution) wanted to transmit it with criticism of the Convention for exceeding its authority and its delegates for violating their instructions only to revise the Articles. In the course of the debate, Antifederalists tried to propose amendments. Richard Henry Lee, Madison's Virginia colleague, proposed a bill of rights and other amendments changing the structure of the Constitution. Madison opposed Lee vigorously and argued that "a bill of rights [was] unnecessary because the powers [of Congress] are enumerated and only extend to certain cases." To add amendments to the Constitution would create insurmountable problems. An amended Constitution would be Congress's Constitution; and, according to the Articles of Confederation, when Congress proposed changes to the Articles, they were to be sent to the state legislatures for their unanimous approval. The Convention, on the other hand, had suggested that the Constitution be sent to the states to be considered in specially elected ratifying conventions; and, that when nine conventions ratified, the Constitution would go into effect among the ratifying states. Thus, Madison said, "There will be two plans. Some [states] will accept one and some another. Confusion would result."[78]

Although they controlled eleven of the twelve state delegations in attendance (Congress voted by states with one vote per state), Federalists were willing to compromise because they wanted to preserve the appearance of unanimity. Congress was, as usual, meeting behind closed doors, and Federalists hoped that neither the discussion in Congress nor Lee's amendments would become known by the public. They agreed to transmit the Constitution to the states without endorsement if Antifederalists would agree to strike any dissent (including Lee's proposed

78. Melancton Smith's Notes of the Debate in Congress, *Constitutional Documents and Records*, 335, 337.

amendments) from the journals. To avoid congressional endorsement, the outnumbered Antifederalists agreed to the compromise. Shrewd politicians that they were, Federalists, led by Madison, cleverly introduced the transmittal resolution with the words "Resolved unanimously," giving the false impression of *unanimous approbation*, while Congress was unanimously agreeing only to send the Constitution to the states for their consideration. When Madison explained to George Washington what had happened in Congress, Washington replied. "I am better pleased that the proceedings of the Convention is handed from Congress by a unanimous vote (feeble as it is) than if it had appeared under stronger marks of approbation without it. This apparent unanimity will have its effect. Not every one has opportunities to peep behind the curtain; and as the multitude often judge from externals, the appearance of unanimity in that body, on this occasion, will be of great importance."[79]

Except for a week's trip to Philadelphia in early November, Madison stayed in New York City to attend Congress and to serve as an unofficial Federalist clearinghouse of information until early March 1788, when he returned to Orange County to stand for election to the Virginia ratifying convention. Letters from Federalists all over the country streamed in to him. He, in turn, gathered and consolidated this information and relayed it to his correspondents throughout the country. Newspapers and pamphlets were sent to him to forward to Hamilton in New York, to Rufus King in Boston, or to Federalists in Virginia. He transmitted copies of the debates from the Pennsylvania and Massachusetts conventions to correspondents. Only two other Federalists performed similar functions—Secretary at War Henry Knox who was also in New York, and Washington at Mount Vernon. Until

79. Washington to Madison, Mount Vernon, October 10, 1787, *Papers of James Madison*, X, 189.

very late in the process, there was no Antifederalist coordination in the campaign against the Constitution.

Antifederalists took the lead in the newspaper debate over whether or not to ratify the Constitution. About a month into the debate, Alexander Hamilton and John Jay decided to write a comprehensive exposition of the Constitution in a series of newspaper essays. They asked Madison to join the enterprise. The purpose of the series was to show the necessity of the Union, the weaknesses of the Articles of Confederation, and the nature and benefits of the new Constitution. The essays were "to give a satisfactory answer to all the objections which shall have made their appearance that may seem to have any claim to the public's attention."[80]

Later in life Madison described how the essays were prepared for publication. The essays

> were written most of them in great haste, and without any special allotment of the different parts of the subject to the several writers. J.M. being at the time a member of the then Congress, and A.H. being also a member, and occupied moreover in his profession at the bar, it was understood that each was to write as their respective situations permitted, preserving as much as possible an order & connection in the papers successively published. This will account for deficiency in that respect, and also for an occasional repetition of the views taken of particular branches of the subject. The haste with which many of the papers were penned, in order to get thro the subject whilst the Constitution was before the public, and to comply with the arrangement by which the printer was to keep his newspaper open

80. DHRC, XIII, 486; Hamilton to George Washington, New York, October 30, 1787, Syrett, *Hamilton*, IV, 306.

for four numbers every week, was such that the performance must have borne a very different aspect without the aid of historical and other notes which have been used in the Convention and without the familiarity with the whole subject produced by the discussions there. It frequently happened that whilst the printer was putting into type the parts of a number, the following parts were under the pen, & to be furnished in time for the press.

In the beginning it was the practice of the writers, of A.H. & J.M. particularly to communicate each to the other, their respective papers before they were sent to the press. This was rendered so inconvenient, by the shortness of the time allowed, that it was dispensed with. Another reason was, that it was found most agreeable to each, not to give a positive sanction to all the doctrines and sentiments of the other; there being a known difference in the general complexion of their political theories.[81]

Madison wrote twenty-nine of the eighty-five essays in the series: Nos. 10, 14, 18–20, 37–58, 62–63. His first essay is the most famous of all the eighty-five. In *The Federalist* 10, published in the New York *Daily Advertiser* on November 22, 1787, Madison deals with special-interest-group politics and how to preserve liberty in a republic. Madison rejected the commonly held belief espoused by the Baron de Montesquieu that republics could survive only in small confined countries with homogeneous populations. Most former republics satisfied these requirements, but they all collapsed and degenerated into despotism. Madison turned Montesquieu's ideas on their head. He argued that to be viable, republics needed both to

81. Elizabeth Fleet, ed., "Madison's Detatched Memoranda," *William and Mary Quarterly*, 3rd ser., III (1946), 565.

expand their territory and to diversify their populations.

Free societies, Madison wrote, would always contain factions—today we call them special-interest groups—which were dedicated to their own interest at the expense of the general good and could be dangerous to the rights of others. But to eliminate factions would require the elimination of liberty. Madison favored creating conditions that would make it difficult for factions to form majorities. The larger the area and the more diversified the population, the greater the difficulty for any majority to be formed or, once formed, of staying together for a long time. "Extend the sphere, and you take in a greater variety of parties and interests; you make it less probable that a majority of the whole will have a common motive to invade the rights of other citizens." Madison expected that under the Constitution there would be struggles among special-interest groups. But they were not to be feared because the Constitution was so constructed that factions would be controlled and prevented from doing harm.

Madison wanted to provide a buffer for federal legislators from the arbitrary and immediate whims of an outraged majority—the most dangerous element in any democratic society. He hoped that America could be ruled by the most meritorious and virtuous citizens, who would compose a "natural aristocracy." He despised government by a hereditary aristocracy—those favored by birth and wealth.

One way to guarantee that only the best people would be elected was to limit the size of Congress. If all the states ratified the Constitution, the first Senate would contain twenty-six members and the first House of Representatives only sixty-five members. Opponents of the Constitution worried that such small legislative bodies could not adequately represent the American people. After all, tiny Rhode Island had an assembly of seventy; while Massachusetts had almost 400 in its House of

Representatives. Madison, however, knew that the small number of federal legislators would require large, perhaps even statewide, election districts in which only the most meritorious could garner enough support to be elected. The small Congress would also provide the corollary benefit of keeping government expenses down.

To further insulate federal legislators, Madison supported longer terms—six years for senators and two years for representatives as opposed to the standard one-year terms in state legislatures and in the Confederation Congress. In addition federal legislators should not be subject to recall, term limits, or binding instructions by their constituents. The per-diem salaries and expenses of federal legislators would also be paid by the federal treasury as opposed to the individual state treasuries under the Articles of Confederation. Knowledgeable representatives would listen to the debate and use their intellect to make the proper choice for their country as well as for their own districts. In *The Federalist* 37 Madison defended the terms for representatives and senators.

> The genius of republican liberty, seems to demand on one side, not only that all power should be derived from the people, but, that those entrusted with it should be kept in dependence on the people, by a short duration of their appointments; and that, even during this short period, the trust should be placed not in a few, but in a number of hands. Stability, on the contrary, requires, that the hands, in which power is lodged, should continue for a length of time the same. A frequent change of men will result from a frequent return of electors, and a frequent change of measures, from a frequent change of men; whilst energy in government requires not only a certain duration of power, but the execution of it by a single hand.

In *The Federalist* 39, Madison showed that the new Constitution was based on republican principles and that the Constitution would create a government that would be partly federal (operating on the states) and partly national (operating directly on the people). Madison defined a republican government as one "which derives all its power directly or indirectly from the great body of the people; and is administered by persons holding their offices during pleasure, for a limited period, or during good behavior." There was no question in Madison's mind that the new federal government would be republican in nature. "No other form," he wrote, "would be reconcilable with the genius of the people of America; with the fundamental principles of the revolution; or with that honorable determination, which animates every votary of freedom, to rest all our political experiments on the capacity of mankind for self-government."

In one of his greatest literary flourishes in *The Federalist* 51, Madison concisely stated the problem faced by all governments. "If men were angels, no government would be necessary. If angels were to govern men, neither external nor internal controls on government would be necessary. In framing a government which is to be administered by men over men, the great difficulty lies in this: You must first enable the government to control the governed; and in the next place oblige it to control itself." Seemingly the Articles of Confederation and many of the state constitutions did neither. All agreed that the central government to be created under the new Constitution would have sufficient power to govern the people. The question was whether it would have sufficient checks to be able to control itself.

The primary method of controlling government, Madison wrote, was through a dependence on people through elections. But since experience had shown that elections alone were inadequate, Madison argued that "auxiliary precautions" were needed. These included fundamental structural safeguards built into the Constitution—separation of powers, checks and balances, a bicameral legislature, and the division of power between state and federal governments. "In the compound republic of America," Madison stated, "the power surrendered by the people is first divided between two distinct governments, and then the portion allotted to each, subdivided among distinct and separate departments. Hence a double security arises to the rights of the people. The different governments will control each other, at the same time that each will be controlled by itself." During the debate over the ratification of the Constitution, Madison argued that it was these structural protections that safeguarded rights, not the "parchment barrier" of a bill of rights. Only after the Constitution had been ratified did Madison enlarge his auxiliary precautions to include a bill of rights.

According to Madison, the most serious constitutional problem facing America was the dominance of state governments. Under the Articles of Confederation, states retained their sovereignty, freedom and independence, and Congress had only those powers expressly delegated to it by the Articles. Congress had no power or authority to restrain what the states did. Madison felt that the states had to be limited so that they could not pass laws that violated the rights of individuals or subverted the authority of the federal government. Article I, section 10 of the Constitution specifically prohibits the states from certain actions, while the supremacy clause in Article VI provides that "This Constitution, and the laws of the United States which shall be made in pursuance thereof; and all treaties made, or which shall be made, under the authority of the United States, shall be the supreme law of the land; and the judges in every state shall be bound thereby, anything in the Constitution or laws of any State to the contrary notwithstanding." Although not as extensive as Madison's proposed congressional veto over any and all state laws, Madison defended the supremacy clause in *The Federalist* 44. Without this clause, he wrote, the Constitution "would have been evidently and radically defective. . . . the world would have seen for the first time, a system of government founded on an inversion of the fundamental principles of all government; it would have seen the authority of the whole society every where subordinate to the authority of the parts; it would have seen a monster, in which the head was under the direction of the members."

In one brief sentence in *The Federalist* 51, Madison explained what the Constitution attempted to do. "Justice," he wrote, "is the end of government." Throughout his writings in *The Federalist*, Madison demonstrated how the Constitution placed restrictions on government so that liberty and justice under a stable government would prevail.

The Federalist was recognized at the time as the definitive explication of the Constitution. George Washington wrote that no other work was "so well calculated . . . to produce conviction on an unbiased mind."[82] Thomas Jefferson told Madison that the series was "the best commentary on the principles of government which ever was written."[83]

THE VIRGINIA RATIFYING CONVENTION

The opposition to the Constitution in Virginia was strong. Edmund Randolph and George Mason had refused to sign the Constitution in the Federal Convention. Other opposition was expected from three former Virginia governors—Patrick Henry, Benjamin Harrison, and Thomas Nelson—as well as from Arthur

82. Washington to Alexander Hamilton, Mount Vernon, August 28, 1788, Syrett, *Hamilton*, V, 207.

83. Jefferson to Madison, Paris, November 18, 1788, *Papers of James Madison*, XI, 353.

and Richard Henry Lee. Against this powerful force, Madison would be the Constitution's "main pillar: but tho an immensely powerful one, it is questionable whether he can bear the weight of such a host." Jefferson also knew that Washington would play a minor role, for "it is not in his character to exert himself much in the case."[84]

Actually Madison did not want to serve in the Virginia ratifying convention. He felt that the final decision on the Constitution "should proceed from men who had no hand in preparing and proposing it."[85] But Madison's fellow Virginia Federalists convinced him that he was needed in the convention. He was the best person to explain what the Federal Convention had done and why. Seeing that other Federal Convention delegates served in their state ratifying conventions also helped persuade Madison to serve. He thus reluctantly agreed to stand for election to the convention from his home of Orange County, but he hoped that he would not have to campaign for a seat. In fact, he expected not to go home from New York for the elections. Friends, however, warned him to return to Virginia. Governor Randolph implored him. "You must come in. Some people in Orange are opposed to your politicks. Your election to the convention is, I believe, sure; but I beg you not to hazard it by being absent at the time."[86] William Moore, a friend and Orange County planter, reminded Madison of "the disadvantage of being absent at Elections to those who offer themselves to serve the Public. I must therefore intreat and conjure you, nay command you, if it was in my Power, to be here in February or the first of March next. If you do, I think your Election will be certain (if not I believe from reports it will be uncertain)."[87]

84. Jefferson to William Carmichael, Paris, December 15, 1787, DHRC, VIII, 241.

85. Madison to Ambrose Madison, New York, November 8, 1787, *Papers of James Madison*, X, 244.

86. Randolph to Madison, Richmond, January 3, 1788, ibid., 350.

87. Moore to Madison, Orange, January 31, 1788, ibid., 454.

Because of "the badness of the roads & some other delays" Madison did not reach Orange until March 23, one day before the elections. Much to his chagrin, he found "the County filled with the most absurd and groundless prejudices against the federal Constitution." For the first time in his life Madison felt compelled "to mount . . . the rostrum before a large body of the people, and to launch into a harangue of some length in the open air and on a very windy day. What the effect might be I cannot say, but either that experiment or the exertion of the federalists or perhaps both, the misconceptions of the Government were so far corrected that two federalists one of them myself were elected by a majority of nearly 4 to one. It is very probable that a very different event would have taken place as to myself if the efforts of my friends had not been seconded by my presence."[88] Another report indicated that Madison had "converted" the people of Orange "in a speech of an hour & three quarters."[89] Francis Taylor, Madison's cousin and an Orange County planter, reported that Madison had received 202 votes, while fellow Federalist James Gordon received 187. The two Antifederalist candidates received 56 and 34 votes.

The Virginia convention met in Richmond from June 2 to June 27. Madison was one of five of Virginia's seven delegates to the Federal Convention who served in the state convention. He led the Federalists with strong assistance from Governor Edmund Randolph, George Nicholas, George Wythe, convention president Edmund Pendleton, and John Marshall. Against them was a pha-lanx of powerful Antifederalists led by Patrick Henry, George Mason, William Grayson, and James Monroe. The stress of combating such dynamic speakers wore heavily on Madison. In fact, for two days (June 9 and 10) he was too sick from stress to attend the convention pro-

88. Madison to Eliza House Trist, Orange, March 25, 1788, ibid., XI, 5–6.

89. James Duncanson to James Maury, Fredericksburg, May 8, 1788, DHRC, IX, 604.

ceedings. Federalists succeeded in getting the convention to agree to examine the Constitution paragraph by paragraph—a procedure conducive to Madison's scholarly style as a speaker. Despite the convention's rule, Henry used his dynamic oratorical dominance over the delegates to denounce the Constitution in broad, general strokes.

Madison responded to virtually all arguments put forth by the Antifederalists. His "plain, ingenious, & elegant reasoning" was repeatedly praised.[90] He decried Henry's generalities. He demanded specifics. Show us, he said, where the dangers are.[91] "It is urged that abuses may happen.—How is it possible to answer objections against [the] possibility of abuses? It must strike every logical reasoner, that these cannot be entirely provided against."[92] Governments must have coercive power. "There never was a Government without force. What is the meaning of Government?" he asked. It is "an institution to make people do their duty. A Government leaving it to do his duty, or not, as he pleases, would be a new species of Government, or rather no Government at all."[93] "We must limit our apprehensions to certain degrees of probability." Many of the Antifederalist evils were "extremely improbable. Nay, almost impossible."[94] "There must be some degree of confidence put in agents [of government], or else we must reject a state of civil society altogether."[95] "If a possibility be the cause of objection, we must object to every Government in America."[96] "If powers be necessary, apparent danger is not a sufficient reason against conceding them."[97]

90. James Breckinridge to John Breckinridge, Richmond, June 13, 1788, ibid., X, 1621.

91. Speech on June 6, 1788, ibid., IX, 989.

92. Speech on June 16, 1788, ibid, X, 1302.

93. Ibid.

94. Ibid., 1319.

95. Speech on June 17, 1788, ibid., 1343.

96. Speech on June 12, 1788, ibid., 1295.

97. Speech on June 6, 1788, ibid., IX, 990.

Madison argued that the Constitution "increases the security of liberty more than any Government that ever was," despite or perhaps because it had power.[98] The Constitution would "promote public happiness."[99] The militia power of Congress would protect states from domestic insurrections and allow the federal government to guarantee the states republican forms government.[100] "Governments destitute of energy," he said, "will ever produce anarchy."[101] Freedom was lost more frequently by having too many freedoms, not from having a government with appropriate powers.[102] Madison opposed a bill of rights because the Constitution would create a government of strictly delegated powers, and the powers it had would not endanger rights. It was not possible to list all the rights the people had, and any right not listed would be presumed to be given up.[103]

The new government's powers were appropriate. The power of laying and collecting taxes was indispensable and essential to the existence of any efficient, well-organized system of government.[104] "Voluntary contributions will eventually end in disunion and Union is indispensably necessary."[105] Madison defended the necessary and proper clause, arguing that the legislative powers were limited and defined.[106] Because the Constitution established a government with only delegated powers, "the delegation alone warrants the exercise of any power."[107] "The powers of the General Government relate to external

98. Speech on June 14, 1788, ibid., X, 1295.

99. Speech on June 6, 1788, ibid., IX, 989.

100. Ibid., 992.

101. Speech on June 7, 1788, ibid., 1031.

102. Speech on June 6, 1788, ibid., 990.

103. Speech on June 24, 1788, ibid., X, 1507.

104. Speech on June 7, 1788, ibid., 1028.

105. Ibid., 1031.

106. Speeches on June 16, 17, and 6, 1788, ibid., 1323, 1340; ibid., IX, 996.

107. Speech on June 24, 1788, ibid., X, 1502.

objects, and are but few. But the powers in the States relate to those great objects which immediately concern the prosperity of the people."[108] "The exercise of the power must be consistent with the object of the delegation."[109]

If people would give "a fair and liberal interpretation upon the words," Madison believed that the Constitution would be found safe.[110] The new government would "not become consolidated as a national government."[111] It would be partly federal and partly national.[112]

The great defect of the Articles of Confederation was that Congress could exercise its powers only over states and not individuals.[113] The Confederation was weak and "foreign nations [were] unwilling to form any treaties with us."[114] The inability of Congress to pay its debts endangered the country's happiness and security.[115] If the Articles of Confederation were not changed, "consequences must ensue that Gentlemen do not now apprehend."[116]

Madison granted that the Constitution was imperfect,[117] but amendments could be obtained when needed and in fact were easier to obtain under the Constitution than under the Confederation.[118] Madison strongly objected to the argument that the Constitution should be amended before Virginia ratified. This was "but another name" for rejection; previous amendments were "pregnant with dreadful dangers"; and they presented "the extreme

108. Speech on June 11, 1788, ibid., IX, 1152.
109. Speech on June 19, 1788, ibid., X, 1396.
110. Speech on June 19, 1788, ibid., 1409.
111. Speech on June 4, 1788, ibid., IX, 941.
112. Speech on June 6, 1788, ibid., 995.
113. Speech on June 7, 1788, ibid., 1029.
114. Ibid., 1034.
115. Ibid., 1035.
116. Ibid., 1033.
117. Speech on June 24, 1788, ibid., X, 1499.
118. Speech on June 6, 1788, ibid., IX, 990–91.

risk of perpetual disunion."[119] How could amendments be obtained before ratification, Madison argued, when Antifederalists could not agree among themselves.[120] The convention should, like other state conventions, recommend amendments to be considered after the Constitution was ratified in the first federal Congress.[121] Madison asked, "If there be an equal zeal in every State [for alterations], can there be a doubt that they will concur in reasonable amendments?"[122]

Madison confessed that "from the first moment that my mind was capable of contemplating political subjects, I never, till this moment, ceased wishing success to a well regulated Republican Government. The establishment of such in America was my most ardent desire."[123] He believed in the "great republican principle, that the people will have virtue and intelligence to select men of virtue and wisdom."[124] "A change" Madison said, was "absolutely necessary." He saw "no danger in submitting to practice an experiment which seems to be founded on the best theoretic principles."[125] It was time to establish a viable republic in America.

Madison told the delegates that America was at a crossroads. "It is a most awful thing that depends on our decision—no less than whether the thirteen States shall Unite freely, peaceably, and unanimously, for the security of their common happiness and liberty, or whether every thing is to be put in confusion and disorder!"[126] "There are uncertainty and confusion on the one hand, and order, tranquility and certainty on the other."[127]

119. Speeches on June 6, 24, 25, 1788, ibid., 994–95; X, 1501, 1503–4, 1518.

120. Speech on June 24, 1788, ibid., 1501.

121. Speech on June 25, 1788, ibid, 1518.

122. Ibid.

123. Speech on June 14, 1788, ibid., 1283.

124. Speech on June 20, 1788, ibid., 1417.

125. Speech on June 14, 1788, ibid., 1283.

126. Speech on June 24, 1788, ibid., 1500.

127. Speech on June 25, 1788, ibid., 1518.

For several weeks it was uncertain whether the convention would adopt the Constitution or reject it. With assurances offered by Madison that Federalists would support recommendatory amendments, the convention voted by a slim majority of 89 to 79 to ratify the Constitution without previous amendments. Two days later the convention recommended that Virginia's future representatives in Congress propose forty amendments—half in the form of a declaration of rights and half structural changes to the Constitution.

Most observers agreed that without Madison, Virginia would not have ratified the Constitution. One spectator in the convention gallery reported that Madison spoke "with such force of reasoning, and a display of irresistible truths, that opposition seemed to have quitted the field."[128] Another report said that "Mr. Henry's declamatory powers [were] vastly overpowered by the deep reasoning of our glorious little Madison."[129] Madison was even praised poetically.

> "*Maddison* among the rest,
> Pouring from his narrow chest,
> More than Greek or Roman sense,
> Boundless tides of eloquence."[130]

Of all the speakers, it was Madison who "carried the votes of the two parties. He was always clear, precise and consistent in his reasoning, and always methodical and pure in his Language."[131]

128. Bushrod Washington to George Washington, Richmond, June 7, 1788, ibid., 1581.

129. "Extract of a letter from Richmond, June 18," *Pennsylvania Mercury*, June 26, 1788, ibid., 1688.

130. "Extract of a letter from a gentleman of the first information, dated Petersburg, June 9, 1788, received per a vessel in 5 days from Norfolk," *Massachusetts Centinel*, June 25, 1788, ibid., 1684.

131. Martin Oster to Comte de Luzerne, Richmond, June 28, 1788, ibid., 1690.

Virginia was the tenth state to ratify. New Hampshire, which ratified four days earlier, had the honor of being the ninth state to ratify and thus implement the Constitution. With Virginia's ratification, New York realized that it must also accept the Constitution and work for amendments within Congress instead of outside of the Union.

THE FIRST FEDERAL ELECTIONS

With the Constitution adopted, attention focused on who would be elected to fill the new federal offices. Virginia Federalists hoped that James Madison would be elected one of the state's first U.S. senators. The Constitution provided that senators were to be elected by the state legislatures. The Virginia legislature decided to elect senators in the same manner in which it had elected delegates to the Confederation Congress—by a joint ballot of both houses. Patrick Henry, the acknowledged leader of the dominant Antifederalists in the legislature, worked strenuously to defeat Madison. Henry "publickly said that no person who wishes the constitution to be amended should vote for Mr. Madison to be in the senate."[132] Henry conceded Madison's "talents and integrity," but argued that he was "unseasonable upon this occasion" because his "federal politics were so adverse to the opinions of many" Virginians. Even Madison's friends admitted that "it was doubtful, whether [he] would obey instructions" to support amendments. "There," said Henry, "the secret is out: it is doubted whether Mr. Madison will obey instructions."[133] Henry Lee wrote Madison that "Mr. Henry on the floor exclaimed against your political character & pro-

132. Charles Lee to George Washington, Richmond, October 29, 1788, Merrill Jensen, Gordon DenBoer et al., eds., *The Documentary History of the First Federal Elections, 1788–1790* (4 vols., Madison, Wis., 1976–), II, 269.

133. Edmund Randolph to James Madison, Richmond, November 10, 1788, *Papers of James Madison*, XI, 339.

nounced you unworthy of the confidence of the people in the station of Senator. That your election would terminate in producing rivulets of blood throughout the land."[134] On November 6, Madison, along with Antifederalists Richard Henry Lee and William Grayson, were nominated for the two senate seats. Two days later, the legislature, under the control of Patrick Henry, voted to elect Lee and Grayson. They received 98 and 86 votes, respectively. Madison received 77 votes.

Federalists throughout the country lamented the loss. A newspaper columnist in Maryland condemned the ". . . misfortune. Mr. Maddison was excluded [from the Senate] who was allowed to be the *greatest man* in the general convention, though only little more than thirty years of age; his abilities are transcendently great, his integrity unimpeached, and he had the honor of first moving for the appointment of a general convention."[135] A week later, the same essayist criticized Patrick Henry for excluding "from the service of his country the ablest statesman in it."[136] Martin Oster, French vice consul in Richmond and Norfolk, reported that "It is generally regretted that Mr. James Madison, a good federalist, is not one of these representatives, because of his outstanding worth."[137] A delegate to the Assembly from Winchester described how Madison was defeated and what it meant for the country.

> Those who know the abilities of Mr. Madison, who know that his whole life has been devoted to the services of the public, and that he has so con-

134. Henry Lee to Madison, Alexandria, November 19, 1788, ibid., XI, 356.

135. "A Marylander," Baltimore *Maryland Gazette,* December 26, 1788, *First Federal Elections,* 156.

136. "A Marylander," Baltimore *Maryland Gazette,* January 2, 1789, ibid., 182.

137. Oster to Comte de la Luzerne, Norfolk, February 11, 1789, ibid., 401.

ducted himself as to avoid every cause of offence in his public speeches and private conversation to any man or description of men—that envy itself, or the jaundiced eye of faction have never imputed to him interested or corrupt motives—might be at a loss to account for such marks of neglect or disapprobation:—But, Sir, the conduct of Mr. Henry on the day of Mr. Madison's nomination, fully explains the mystery—in a well informed speech, he made a pointed attack against him in the House, taking for the ground of his opposition, Mr. Madison's attachment to the Federal Government. I felt much for Mr. Madison, but more for my country—for I considered this as the trumpet of discord—a dæmon which I fear will destroy that domestic peace and happiness which unanimity of sentiment has hitherto secured to us, as well during the late arduous conflict as since its happy conclusion.—Hereafter, when a gentleman is nominated to a public office, it is not his virtue, his abilities or his patriotism we are to regard, but whether he is a federalist or anti-federalist—a distinction which might well take place while the new government was under consideration, but which ought to cease as soon as it was agreed to.[138]

After Madison's rejection as a senator, he and his fellow Virginia Federalists attempted to get him elected to the U.S. House of Representatives. On November 19, the

138. Extract of a letter from a Member of the Assembly at Richmond, to his correspondent in this town, dated Nov. 8, 1788, Winchester *Virginia Centinel*, November 19, 1788, ibid., 379. The letter writer was probably Alexander White, a delegate to the Assembly from Winchester. He had predicted that Madison would be defeated "notwithstanding his great abilities, his virtue, and his respectful polite behaviour to all men of all Parties." To Mary Wood, Richmond, November 5, 1788, ibid., 273.

Virginia legislature created ten election districts throughout the state and called for the election to be held on
February 2, 1789. Patrick Henry's influence was again pre-
dominant, and he did what he could to defeat Madison's
candidacy. The election law provided that candidates had
to be residents of the district they represented. Henry
thereupon loaded district five (Madison's home district)
with eight counties, half of which were heavily
Antifederalist. Antifederalists selected James Monroe,
Madison's close friend who had staunchly opposed the
ratification of the Constitution in the state convention,
as Madison's only challenger. It was expected that
Monroe's supporters would be "most active . . . to secure
his election."[139]

Madison's friends advised him that his election would
not be easy. They strongly advised him to return home
and campaign throughout the district, appearing in each
county on its monthly court day or to write a statement
for publication outlining his position on amendments to
the Constitution. Madison "always despised and wish[ed]
to shun" "electioneering appearances." Before he knew
what counties formed his district, Madison felt that "If
Orange should fall into a federal district it is probable I
shall not be opposed; if otherwise a successful opposition
seems unavoidable."[140] But the news from the fifth district was bad. Antifederalists, encouraged by Patrick
Henry, were "making every exertion, however unmanly to
exclude" Madison from the House of Representatives.[141]
They

> propagate an idea that you are wholly opposed to
> any alteration in the Govt. having declared that

139. Hardin Burnley to Madison, Richmond, December 16, 1788,
ibid., 328.

140. James Madison to Edmund Randolph, Philadelphia,
November 23, 1788, ibid., 320.

141. Richard Bland Lee to Madison, Richmond, November 25, 1788,
ibid., 321.

you did not think that a single letter in it would admit of a change. This circumstance alone would render your presence necessary for let these reports be denied as often as they may by your friends, there are others among those who oppose you who will as repeatedly revive them and nothing can give them an effectual check but a Denial of them in the face of the people and an avowal of your real Sentiments on the subject of Amendments.[142]

A few Virginia Federalists advised Madison not to make the arduous journey home to campaign. They expected that he would be elected in his home district, because they had been told that "the people of both descriptions are much disgusted with all the proceedings of the Anti's here." If Madison were defeated in district five, Virginia Federalists would run him as a candidate in either district three or district ten. Although this would violate the state election law, which required that candidates be a "bona fide" resident of the district, Madison's advisers were "of the opinion that such a restriction was not within the power of the Legislature, and that it will avail nothing in Congress, where the qualifications of Members are to be judged of."[143]

Campaigning was heavy in district 5 throughout January 1789. Newspapers, broadsides, and personal visits one-on-one got the candidates' messages across. Monroe's supporters advocated that voters "unite in favor of a Gentleman who has been uniformly in favour of Amendments. . . . A man who possesses great abilities, integrity and a most amiable Character who has been many years a member of Congress, of the House of Delegates and of the Privy Council." They said, the ques-

142. Hardin Burnley to Madison, Richmond, December 16, 1788, ibid., 328–29.

143. Edward Carrington to Madison, Richmond, December 2, 1788, ibid., 322. See also Alexander White to Madison, Richmond, December 4, 1788, ibid., 323.

tion voters should ask themselves was: Do you favor amendments to the Constitution? "If you do, who is the most likely to obtain them, the man who has been uniformly in favor of them, or one who has been uniformly against them."[144]

Madison was so concerned about the election that he returned to Virginia late in December to campaign. He attended January court days and met and corresponded with county leaders and influential Baptist ministers. He and Monroe traveled around the district together and on several occasions they debated. At one such debate on the court day in Culpeper County, "in the open air, on a cold, January day . . . in the face of a keen, north-easterly wind" one of Madison's ears suffered frostbite. Traces of the injury remained throughout Madison's life. He sometimes "playfully pointed to them as the honorable scars he had borne from the battle-field."[145]

Madison wrote several letters that were published to explain his position on amendments. To Baptist minister George Eve, the pastor of Blue Run Church in Orange County, he wrote:

> I freely own that I have never seen in the Constitution as it now stands those serious dangers which have alarmed many respectable Citizens. Accordingly whilst it remained unratified, and it was necessary to unite the States in some one plan, I opposed all previous alterations as calculated to throw the States into dangerous contentions, and to furnish the Secret enemies of the Union with an opportunity of promoting its dissolution. Circumstances are now changed. The Constitution is established on the ratifications of eleven States and a very great majority of the peo-

144. An Appeal for the Election of James Monroe, c. January 1789, ibid., 329–30.

145. Quoted from William C. Rives, *History of the Life and Times of James Madison* (3 vols., Boston, 1866–68), II, 656–57.

ple of America; and amendments, if pursued with a proper moderation and in a proper mode, will be not only safe, but may serve the double purpose of satisfying the minds of well meaning opponents, and of providing additional guards in favour of liberty. Under this change of circumstances, it is my sincere opinion that the Constitution ought to be revised, and that the first Congress meeting under it, ought to prepare and recommend to the States for ratification, the most satisfactory provisions for all essential rights, particularly the rights of Conscience in the fullest latitude, the freedom of the press, trials by jury, security against general warrants &c.[146]

A friend to religious freedom addressed the freeholders of the district.

The eyes of all America have been fixed on Virginia, with anxious expectation, that in her late choice of senators, the eminent services and distinguished virtue of Mr. MADISON, would not have been forgot. The eyes of all virtuous in Virginia, are now placed on you, with confident hopes, that you will not frustrate their warmest wish, by following the example of your Legislature. Remember, it is now no novelty for the people to correct the errors of the Assembly, and recal them to a sense of their duty. It is, indeed, the most valuable prerogative which a free people can enjoy, and, when manfully asserted, will never fail to prove their defence against every violation of their rights, arising either from party spirit, or the overgrown influence of individuals.
    . . . Believe me, you were never called on to give your votes on a matter of such infinite con-

146. Madison to George Eve, Orange, January 2, 1789, *First Federal Elections*, II, 330–31.

cern. It is not every age, nor every country, which can furnish a man of equal endowments and virtues with the one you have it in your power to chuse. Virginia cannot boast his equal. What then must be the anguish of mind, which the lovers of virtue, morality and religious freedom, through the state, will suffer, if you disappoint them in a man whom they revere as the fairest patron of the former, and the firmest bulwark of the latter?"[147]

Madison's effort paid off. The polls opened on Monday, February 2, under severe winter conditions. Temperatures fell to −10° below zero that morning. A few votes trickled in over the next couple days. Madison and Monroe evenly split the eight counties of district five, but Madison had a 336 vote majority out of the 2,280 votes cast. Madison's cousin, the Reverend James Madison, president of the College of William and Mary, expressed the feelings of many Virginians. "I rejoice that you are in a Situation, which enables you to be extensively useful, & that, we who are to receive the Law may at least be assured, one Voice will always utter what Wisdom & Virtue shall dictate."[148] South Carolinian Ralph Izard was "very glad to find that Mr. Madison is elected. . . . I think highly of his abilities and expect considerable advantages will be derived from them."[149] Cyrus Griffin, a Virginian and the last president of the Confederation Congress, wrote Madison that "We all rejoice greatly at your election: indeed, my dear sir, we consider you as the main pillar of the business on the right side."[150]

147. Fredericksburg *Virginia Herald*, January 15, 1789, ibid., 336–37.

148. The Rev. James Madison to Madison, Williamsburg, March 1, 1789, *Papers of James Madison*, XI, 454.

149. Ralph Izard to Thomas Jefferson, Charleston, S.C., April 3, 1789, *Jefferson Papers*, XV, 22.

150. Cyrus Griffin to Madison, New York, April 14, 1789, *Papers of James Madison*.

THE PRESIDENT'S ADVISER

Madison and George Washington first met in August 1781. Their correspondence and collaboration increased in the mid–1780s and they became close friends. Their "relationship flourished because each possessed something the other needed. Washington relied heavily on Madison's advice, pen, and legislative skills. Madison, in turn, found Washington's prestige essential for achieving his goals for the new nation, especially a stronger federal government."[151] For fifteen years their careers intertwined: both left federal service to return to Virginia in 1783, both served in the Federal Convention in Philadelphia in 1787, both took office under the new Constitution in 1789, and both retired from public service in 1797, by which time they were estranged and never communicated with each other again.

When Madison came back to Virginia to campaign for a seat in the House of Representatives, he stopped at Mount Vernon for a week of consultations. After the election, Madison left Montpelier in mid–February 1789 to attend Congress in New York City. On his way, he again stopped at Mount Vernon for ten days. For the next several years, Madison would serve as a special adviser to the president—as a sort of cabinet secretary without portfolio, a floor leader, or almost a prime minister. The president sought Madison's advice on a wide range of issues—on protocol, on appointments, on speeches, on legislation, on foreign affairs, on western lands, and especially on precedent-setting matters. The first service offered by Madison was writing Washington's inaugural address.

Sometime before December 1788, Washington asked David Humphreys, a former aide-de-camp who had been living at Mount Vernon since October 1787, to write an

151. Stuart Leibiger, *Founding Friendship: George Washington, James Madison, and the Creation of the American Republic* (Charlottesville, 1999), 1.

inaugural address in case it might be needed. In early January 1789, when Madison had only recently arrived in Virginia to campaign, Washington sent him a 73-page, handwritten copy of Humphreys' draft. Madison and other confidants confirmed Washington's suspicion that Humphrey's draft ought not to be delivered. Instead, Washington asked Madison to draft a new inaugural address. The two men discussed what should go into the speech.

George Washington took the oath of office as president on the balcony of Federal Hall in New York City on April 30, 1789. After the oath, Washington addressed a joint session of Congress in the Senate chamber. Washington spoke for eleven minutes—far more appropriate than the two hours that it would have taken to deliver Humphreys' version. In the speech Washington expressed his unwillingness and his lack of qualifications to serve as president. A sense of duty—one of the themes of the address—however, forced him to accept the position. "I was summoned by my Country, whose voice I can never hear but with veneration and love." In this his "first official Act," Washington thanked God for smiling upon America, though he never used the word "God." Americans had set an example of adopting a new form of government peacefully. Washington hoped that the members of Congress would work for the good of the Union, because "the preservation of the sacred fire of liberty, and the destiny of the Republican model of Government, are justly considered as *deeply*, perhaps as *finally* staked, on the experiment entrusted to the hands of the American people." The address avoided specific recommendations, with one exception. Washington asked that Congress propose a bill of rights to be added to the Constitution. Such a proposal would demonstrate "a reverence for the characteristic rights of freemen, and a regard for the public harmony."[152]

152. Washington's final inaugural address appears in the *Washington Papers, Presidential Series*, II, 173–77.

The two houses broke up and reassembled in their own chambers. Each house appointed a committee to respond to the president's speech. Madison chaired the House committee. The House vowed to work with the president "in a system of legislation, founded on the principles of an honest policy, and directed by the spirit of a diffusive patriotism."[153] Immediately on receiving the House's response, Washington asked Madison to write his response to the House.[154] Madison's response for Washington said that "Your very affectionate Address produces emotions which I know not how to express."[155] The president was speechless—yes, Madison was doing all of the writing. The Senate responded to the inaugural address on May 16, and again the president asked Madison if he would write his response, which ended with the statement, "I readily engage with you in the arduous, but pleasing, task, of attempting to make a Nation happy."[156] In fact, it could be said that this was Madison's life work—"to make a nation happy."

THE FIRST FEDERAL CONGRESS

Madison arrived in New York in mid–March 1789, but the House of Representatives did not have a quorum until April 1. Much was expected of the new Congress, and much of Madison personally. Fisher Ames, a young dynamic congressman from Massachusetts, said of Madison, "He is our first man."[157] An older Pennsylvania congressman was pleased to see Ames and Madison "introduced to each other—two young but shining polit-

153. U.S. House of Representatives to President George Washington, New York, May 5, 1789, *Washington Papers, Presidential Series*, II, 214–15.

154. Washington to Madison, New York, May 5, ibid, 216–17.

155. Washington to the U.S. House of Representatives, New York, May 8, 1789, ibid., 232.

156. Washington to the U.S. Senate, New York, May 18, 1789, ibid., 324.

157. Ames to George R. Minot, New York, May 3, 1789, Seth Ames, ed., *Works of Fisher Ames* (2 vols., Boston, 1854), I, 35.

ical characters, who cannot fail distinguishing themselves in the Federal legislature."[158] Ames described Madison as

> a man of sense, reading, address, and integrity, as 'tis allowed. Very much Frenchified in his politics. He speaks low, his person is little and ordinary. He speaks decently, as to manner, and no more. His language is very pure, perspicuous, and to the point. Pardon me, if I add, that I think him a little too much of a book politician, and too timid in his politics, for prudence and caution are opposites of timidity. He is not a little of a Virginian, and thinks that state the land of promise, but is afraid of their state politics, and of his popularity there, more than I think he should be. [159]

Two weeks later, Ames again wrote that

> Madison is cool, and has an air of reflection, which is not very distant from gravity and self-sufficiency. In speaking, he never relaxes into pleasantry, and discovers little . . . warmth of heart. . . . he speaks very slow, and his discourse is strongly marked. He states a principle and deduces consequences, with clearness and simplicity. Sometimes declamation is mingled with argument, and he appears very anxious to carry a point by other means than addressing their understandings. He appeals to popular topics, and to the pride of the House, such as that they have voted before, and will be inconsistent. I think him a good man and an able man, but he

158. Henry Wynkoop to Reading Beatty, New York, March 18, 1789, Charlene Bangs Bickford et al., eds., *Documentary History of the First Federal Congress* (Baltimore, 1972–), *Correspondence*, XV, 77.

159. Fisher Ames to George R. Minot, New York, May 3, 1789, *Ames*, I, 35.

has rather too much theory, and wants [i.e., lacks]
that discretion which men of business commonly have. He is also very timid, and seems evidently to want manly firmness and energy of
character.[160]

Ames had some insight into Madison, and his descriptions of his speaking style are valuable. But he greatly
underestimated the steel in Madison and his leadership
ability. In the coming years, Ames and Madison were to
become leaders of their respective parties in the new, often
bitterly partisan party system.

While waiting for a quorum to arrive, Madison read
a list of those elected to Congress, he lamented that there
was but "a very scanty proportion who will share in the
drudgery of business."[161] As in the old Congress, he knew
he would have to take the lead. He did so almost immediately, proposing an impost bill that would provide the
primary revenue for the new government. He opposed a
protective tariff that would help infant American indus-
tries, preferring instead a tariff that would raise enough
revenue to eliminate the need for other taxes and excises.
He also fought strenuously to include a discriminatory
provision in the bill that would levy a higher tariff on the
goods of those countries that did not have commercial
treaties with the United States—a measure aimed primarily at Great Britain. The Senate removed this last
provision.

Madison also began the process of creating the government of the United States. He introduced legislation
to create cabinet departments for foreign affairs, the treasury, and war. In debate, Madison strongly advocated that
the president had the power to remove officials without

160. Fisher Ames to George R. Minot, New York, May 18, 1789,
ibid., 42.
161. Madison to Edmund Randolph, March 1, 1789, *Papers of James
Madison*, XI, 453.

the need for senatorial approval, a position approved by the House and then by the Senate, with Vice President John Adams casting a tie-breaking vote.

Early in the session, Madison announced that he would soon propose amendments to the Constitution. He found little support. Both Federalist and Antifederalist congressmen believed that there were more important matters that needed immediate attention. Undismayed, Madison persevered and on June 8, 1789, presented one of the greatest speeches in congressional history advocating a series of amendments protecting rights. Madison preferred that the amendments be incorporated into the existing text of the Constitution, not collected at the end of the Constitution in the form of a bill of rights.

Madison declared that his purpose in proposing the amendments was to show that Federalists "were as sincerely devoted to liberty and a republican government, as those who charged them with wishing the adoption of this constitution in order to lay the foundation of an aristocracy of despotism." He also wanted to reconcile Antifederalists, the greatest part of whom had opposed the Constitution because it did not contain "those safeguards which they have been long accustomed to have interposed between them and the magistrates who exercised the sovereign powers." He expected that the amendments might also encourage North Carolina and Rhode Island to ratify the Constitution. Madison also believed that a bill of rights would "kill the opposition everywhere" and would eliminate any possibility that a second constitutional convention would be called.

Madison reiterated many things that he stated in his published campaign letters. He never saw the Constitution as dangerous without a bill of rights, but he had opposed any effort to amend the Constitution before it was ratified. Now with the Constitution ratified, he supported amendments to protect rights, but he was "unwilling to see a door opened for a re-consideration of the whole structure of government," as might happen in a second general convention.

Madison argued that in republics, the legislative branch of government "is the most powerful, and most likely to be abused." The great danger was that the majority of the people would through the legislature abuse the rights of the minority. The legislature could be constrained by bicameralism and by the presidential veto. Another powerful restraint would come from the courts through judicial review. By having rights spelled out in the Constitution, "independent tribunals of justice" would draw upon them and "would become an impenetrable bulwark" against every assumption of power in the legislative or executive. The judiciary would strike down as null and void any act of Congress that violated the bill of rights.

Madison always believed that the states had been violating private rights during the Confederation years, and would likely continue to do so. He therefore provided in his amendments that the states could not violate the freedom of conscience, freedom of the press, and the right to trial by jury in criminal cases. During the debate in the House, the right of freedom of speech was added. Later, when the Senate considered the amendments submitted by the House, the amendments limiting the states were deleted. The Senate—elected by the state legislatures at that time—wanted no restrictions on its constituents. Thus, the bill of rights, until after the adoption of the Fourteenth Amendment, applied only to the federal government.

> Madison concluded his speech by saying that nothing is in contemplation, so far as I have mentioned, that can endanger the beauty of the government in any one important feature, even in the eyes of its most sanguine admirers. I have proposed nothing that does not appear to me as prop-

er in itself, or eligible as patronized by a reasonable number of our fellow citizens; and if we can make the constitution better in the opinion of those who are opposed to it, without weakening its frame, or abridging its usefulness, in the judgment of those who are attached to it, we act the part of wise and liberal men to make such alterations as shall produce that effect.... We should obtain the confidence of our fellow citizens, in proportion as we fortify the rights of the people against the encroachments of the government.

The House debated Madison's amendments for two months, deciding to keep them as a separate bill rather than integrating them into the original Constitution. They were thus sent on to the Senate. The Senate modified some amendments and deleted those restricting the states. A conference committee worked out the differences, and the amendments were sent to the states for their consideration. Two years later, the required three-quarters of the state legislatures adopted the ten amendments that we now refer to as the Bill of Rights.

Madison was severely condemned for his staunch advocacy of the amendments during the long House debate. Theodore Sedgwick, a Massachusetts representative, wrote that "Mr. Madison's talents, respectable as they are will for some time be lost to the public, from his timidity. He is constantly haunted with the ghost of Patrick Henry. No man, in my opinion, in this country has more fair and honorable intentions, or more ardently wishes the prosperity of the public, but unfortunately he has not that strength of nerves which will enable him to set at defiance popular and factious clamors."[162] Fisher Ames said that Virginia's "murmurs, if louder than a whis-

---

162. Theodore Sedgwick to Benjamin Lincoln, New York, July 19, 1789, *First Federal Congress: Correspondence*, XVI, 1075.

per, make Mr. Madison's heart quake."[163] Robert Morris, one of Pennsylvania's senators, lamented

> Poor Madison took one wrong step in Virginia by publishing a letter respecting *Amendments* and you, who know every thing, must know what a Cursed thing it is to write *a Book*. He in consequence has been obliged to bring on the proposition for making Amendments; The Waste of precious time is what has vexed me the most, for as to the Nonsense they call Amendments I never expect that any part of it will go through the various Trials which it must pass before it can become a part of the Constitution.[164]

In the old Congress and in the debate over ratifying the new Constitution, Madison had worked closely with Alexander Hamilton. In the new government, it was said that Madison was responsible for Hamilton's being appointed secretary of the treasury. There was every reason to believe that their cooperation would continue. Soon Secretary Hamilton submitted his economic plans for the nation. They called for the wartime debt to be funded at face value to the domestic and foreign holders of government securities of all kinds, the assumption of the states' wartime debt by the federal government, the creation of a national bank with private and public ownership of bank stock, an excise tax on a variety of commodities including whiskey, and a series of bounties and protections for certain manufactures. Madison opposed all of these proposals, which were extremely unpopular in Virginia and in the South. The bank and the bounties, Madison argued, were unconstitutional because they were

---

163. Fisher Ames to George R. Minot, New York, July 2, 1789, ibid., 915.

164. Robert Morris to Richard Peters, New York, August 24, 1789, ibid., 1392.

not powers specifically enumerated in the Constitution. The funding of the debt and the establishment of the bank were adopted despite Madison's opposition. The assumption of the state debts passed in a compromise brokered by Madison, Jefferson, and Hamilton exchanging Southern votes (though not Madison's) in favor of assumption for Northern votes to move the location of the federal capital from New York City to a site along the Potomac River. The support for manufacturing was never enacted.

Madison's opposition to Hamilton's program was severely criticized. He "disgusted many of his friends" as well as his political opponents.[165] According to Theodore Sedgwick:

> Mr. Madison who is the leader of the opposition is an apostate from all his former principles. Whether he is really a convert to anti-federalism—whether he is actuated by the mean and base motives of acquiring popularity in his own state that he may fill the place of Senator which will probably soon be vacated by the death of Grayson, or whether he means to put himself at the head of the discontented in America time will discover. The last, however, I do not suspect, because I have ever considered him as a very timid man. Deprived of his aid the party would soon be weak and inefficient.[166]

Benjamin Goodhue, a Massachusetts congressman, believed that "Madison would be an excellent politician if he was not so much warped by local considerations, and popular influences, but with those about him he is a dangerous foe, to those measures which soar above trifling objects, and have national advantages for their

165. Andrew Craigie to Daniel Parker, New York, May 5, 1790, ibid.
166. Theodore Sedgwick to Pamela Sedgwick, March 4, 1790, ibid.

basis."[167] John Trumbull of Connecticut felt that "Maddison's character is certainly not rising in the public estimation. He now acts on a conspicuous stage and does not equal expectation. He becomes more and more a Southern Partisan and loses his assumed candor and moderation."[168] Gouverneur Morris, a colleague from the Federal Convention, believed that Madison had really hurt his own reputation.

> I am very sorry indeed to learn that our friend Madison has adopted such singular Ideas respecting the public Debt. This Thing will prove injurious to him because it will give a Handle to those who may wish to call his Judgment in Question and the World is so formed that Objections on that Ground are frequently more fatal than upon that of Morals. I think that on this Occasion he has been induced to adopt the Opinions of others for I cannot believe that his own Mind would so much have misled him. I am very very sorry for it because I think he is one of those Men whose Character is valuable to America.[169]

THE OPPOSITION

The politics of the 1790s became increasingly partisan. Thomas Jefferson had come home from Paris late in 1789 and accepted Washington's appointment as U.S. secretary of state. Henry Knox served as secretary of war and Edmund Randolph was attorney general. With the establishment of the cabinet, President Washington gradually relied more on it and less on Madison for advice. Madison

167. Benjamin Goodhue to Samuel Phillips, New York, March 14, 1790, ibid.

168. John Trumbull to John Adams, June 5, 1790, Adams Family Papers, Massachusetts Historical Society.

169. Gouverneur Morris to Robert Morris, London, May 3, 1790.

and Jefferson increasingly felt that Hamilton's policies would lead either to monarchy or a rapprochement with Great Britain. The French Revolution and the European war added to the partisanship as it divided the country. "Democratic-Republican" societies sprang up throughout the country criticizing the influence of Hamilton over the president. The Jay Treaty (1794) with Great Britain further heightened opposition to the Washington administration.

Washington had wanted to retire from the presidency after one term. At Washington's request, Madison had drafted a farewell address for the president. Washington's advisers all convinced him to stay for another term. By 1796, however, Washington was convinced that he would not seek a third term. By this time Washington and Madison had become estranged. The president gave Hamilton Madison's draft 1792 farewell address to recast for publication in September 1796. Both Washington and Madison retired from public service in March 1797 and returned to Virginia.

It was during the beginning of Washington's second term that a major alteration in Madison's personal life occurred. In May 1794 he asked Aaron Burr to formally introduce him to one of his law clients—the attractive twenty-six-year-old widow Dolley Payne Todd. The previous year had been disastrous for Dolley and many others in Philadelphia. Her Quaker husband and in-laws and her youngest child all died in the terrible yellow fever epidemic that struck the city. With the estates settled, Dolley, with one son, was a very eligible widow. Madison was quite smitten with Dolley. She was vivacious, witty, intelligent, and well read. Madison probably also felt more responsibility for Montpelier with the death of his brother Ambrose in 1793 and with his father's advancing age. By August 1794 Dolley had accepted Madison's proposal of marriage. The couple was wed on September 15, 1794. Marriage readily agreed with Madison. Connecticut

Federalist Jonathan Trumbull, Jr. wrote that "Mr. Madison has been married in the course of last summer—which event or some other, has relieved him of much Bile—and rendered him much more open and conversant than I have seen him before."[170]

Vice President John Adams succeeded Washington as president, but his administration drifted deeper into partisan politics and the Federalist party itself divided between supporters of Hamilton and backers of President Adams. An undeclared naval war with France developed after the French, viewing the Jay Treaty as a rapprochement between America and Great Britain, began seizing American merchantmen. The French aggression frightened Federalists who had for several years pictured Jeffersonian Republicans as Jacobins bent on bringing class warfare and the guillotine to America. Jeffersonians increasingly viewed Federalists as monarchists. War fever increased the Federalists' popularity and their majority in Congress.

Congress authorized a provisional army of 25,000 men. President Adams named Washington commander-in-chief; Washington accepted the position on the condition that Hamilton be put second in command. Republicans feared that the army, with Hamilton commanding in the field, would be used not against an invading French army, but against Republicans. The Alien and Sedition Acts of 1798 increased their fears, especially when the administration and the federal judiciary vigorously prosecuted Republican newspaper printers and even one opposition congressman under the Sedition Act.

Madison and Jefferson anonymously wrote resolutions for the Virginia and Kentucky legislatures (both controlled by Jeffersonians) condemning the Alien and Sedition Acts and calling upon the states to work for their repeal. Madison had come a long way in the last decade.

170. Quoted in Ketcham, *James Madison: A Biography*, 387.

In 1787–1788 he saw the states as the greatest danger to the authority of Congress and to the rights of the people. Now, in 1798, he called upon the states to protect the people from the increasingly powerful and despotic federal government.

With war seemingly inevitable, President Adams made one last effort at peace. While this effort ultimately avoided all-out war, it bitterly divided the Federalist Party. And as the threat of war subsided, Federalist war measures, including new taxes, became very unpopular. Jeffersonians strenuously campaigned in 1800 and were highly successful at the state and federal levels. Jefferson and Aaron Burr defeated Adams and Charles Cotesworth Pinckney for the presidency. Although Jefferson was the assumed candidate for president and Burr for vice president, the two men each received 73 electoral votes. Because of the tie vote, the election went to the Federalist-dominated House of Representatives, where it took thirty-six ballots before Jefferson was elected president.

SECRETARY OF STATE

A couple of weeks before the House of Representatives elected Jefferson president, Jefferson asked Madison to come to Washington, D.C., to be his secretary of state. Madison felt such a journey would be premature. Furthermore, on February 27, 1801, after a year during which both Madison and his father were often ill, Madison's father died. As executor of the estate, Madison struggled to fulfill his father's wishes. The settlement was complicated by the fact that, since his father wrote his will years before, two of Madison's siblings had died. Several scraps of paper and a number of oral statements made by James Madison, Sr., also had to be considered. Then, as Madison was about ready to leave Montpelier, he was bed-ridden for four days by a severe attack of rheumatism. Madison finally arrived in the capital city on May 1, 1801. Although nearly half of the country felt that Jefferson was unqualified to be president, "the virtuous, whatever their political Sentiments may be" had confidence in Madison's "Virtue & Talent."[171]

Immediately Madison plunged into his work. The state department not only managed the country's foreign affairs corresponding with America's five ministers, twenty-five consuls, and seven commissioners, but the secretary of state also handled important domestic functions, such as granting copyrights and patents, supervising the mint, administering the coast guard, publishing laws, corresponding with state and territorial governors, and preparing commissions for all presidential appointments. Furthermore, Madison was President Jefferson's closest and most trusted adviser.

Madison spent most of his time dealing with foreign affairs. Immediately he faced a number of crises. Tripoli, which along with Algiers, had signed a treaty with the United States in 1796, broke away from its subservience to Algiers, revoked the treaty, and, in September 1800, captured an American merchantman. The ship was brought to Tripoli and promptly released, but the pasha demanded that America pay Tripoli an annual tribute of $20,000. The newly arrived secretary of state advised the president to send a naval squadron to the Mediterranean without the approval of Congress and openly declare America's intent. Opponents in Congress objected to this executive action, which, in their opinion, was an unconstitutional act of declaring war—a power the Constitution gave exclusively to Congress. Secretary Madison publicly and privately announced the purpose of the naval expedition. It was not to declare war. It was to strengthen the diplomatic leverage of the American consuls in the

171. William Thornton to James Madison, Washington, March 16, 1801, Robert J. Brugger et al., eds., *The Papers of James Madison, Secretary of State Series* (Charlottesville, Va., 1986), I, 24.

Barbary States, to preserve the peace as well as to enhance "the dignity and interests of the United States."[172] The ships' commanders were ordered not to fire unless first fired upon. If Tripoli's navy attacked American vessels, that would be a declaration of war to which the American squadron would be forced to respond.

War ensued and, after some initial success, bogged down for four years. Jefferson and Madison were roundly condemned for their war and for sending insufficient forces to defeat Tripoli quickly. The administration's excessive frugality had prolonged the conflict and endangered American lives.[173] By 1805 the pasha realized the war with America was counterproductive and he signed a peace treaty. Treaties were also signed with Algiers and Tunis. The United States was the only commercial nation whose ships could sail safely in the region without paying tribute.

A more serious diplomatic problem arose when in October 1802 Spain announced the closing of the port of New Orleans to American trade. Under President Washington, a treaty with Spain had formally opened the Mississippi River and the port of New Orleans to American navigation. Unbeknownst to Americans, Spain and France (now allies fighting Great Britain) had secretly agreed to transfer all of the Louisiana territory from Spanish to French control. Napoleon dreamed of recreating the French empire in the Western Hemisphere, and the Spanish saw the French possession as an effective buffer separating Spain's lucrative Mexican colonies from the dangerous, ever-expanding American settlements. Jefferson and Madison viewed the transfer of Louisiana from the weak and ineffective Spanish rule to France as a

172. Madison to James Leander Cathcart, U.S. Consul at Tripoli, Washington, May 21, 1801, ibid., 211.

173. Everett Somerville Brown, ed., *William Plumer's Memorandum of Proceedings in the Senate*, 1803–1807 (New York, 1923), December 31, 1804, pp. 234–35.

danger. Madison instructed Robert R. Livingston, America's new minister to France, to make an offer "on convenient terms" to purchase New Orleans and Florida as the means to end one of America's most "perplexing" problems.[174] The goal was to have "a pacific policy" and "to seek by just means the establishment of the Mississippi, down to its mouth" as America's boundary.[175]

As diplomatic negotiations continued, war fever raged in the American West and a grand French army sent to protect the new French holdings was decimated by rebellious slaves and fever in Santo Domingo. In need of money to carry on his European wars, Napoleon offered to sell America the entire Louisiana territory stretching over 1,000 miles from the Mississippi River to the Rocky Mountains for $15 million. Uncertain of the constitutionality of buying territory from another country, Jefferson thought about seeking a constitutional amendment to authorize the purchase. Madison, however, advised against such a time-consuming action. The treaty power of the president provided sufficient authority for this grand purchase. If Jefferson felt some constitutional qualms when new states were ready to be admitted to the union, a constitutional amendment could be sought at that time. Satisfied with Madison's advice, Jefferson authorized the purchase, creating for America an "empire for liberty." Opposition to the purchase arose in Congress, especially from New England Federalists who saw their region's relative strength in the Union weakened by such an immense acquisition of territory in which slavery might be permitted. The Senate ratified the treaty on October 20, 1803, by a vote of 24 to 7.

The Spanish were quite upset with the sale of

174. To Robert R. Livingston, Department of State, October 15, 1802, January 18, 1803, Mary A. Hackett et al., eds., *The Papers of James Madison, Secretary of State Series* (Charlottesville, 1998), IV, 25, 259.

175. Madison to Robert R. Livingston and James Monroe, Department of State, March 2, 1803, ibid., 364–65.

Louisiana to the United States. The Marquis de Casa Yrujo, Spanish minister to the United States, protested that the sale violated the agreement between Spain and France, thus rescinding the Spanish cession to France. Yrujo also vehemently rejected America's assertion that West Florida was included in the sale. Madison strenuously rejected the Spanish arguments, informing Yrujo "that we shall not withhold any means that may be rendered necessary to secure our object." Troops were sent and America took formal possession of Louisiana on December 20. Insisting on the eastern boundary of Louisiana to the Perdido River (now the western border of the state of Florida), Madison sent James Monroe and Charles Pinckney to Madrid to negotiate a treaty with Spain. No agreement was reached.

Jefferson's second administration was dominated by European affairs. After a brief truce in 1802, the ten-year-old European war was rekindled. As the war intensified, both Britain and France preyed on American shipping. Wanting to avoid war at almost any cost, Jefferson and Madison used commerce—including an embargo on American shipping—as diplomatic leverage to moderate French and British naval aggression against neutral shipping. Nothing was achieved except economic hardship within America, large-scale smuggling of American goods out of the country, and political opposition soaring to new heights in New England. Mathew Carey, a prominent Philadelphia printer, reported that had Jefferson been a Nero and Madison a Caligula, they could not have been "more completely abhorred & detested" than they were in New England.[176] Increasingly throughout his second term, and especially after 1807 when Jefferson announced that he would not seek reelection, the president deferred to his secretary of state, whom he hoped would succeed him. Opponents said "the President wants

176. To James Madison, Philadelphia, August 12, 1812, Robert A. Rutland et al., eds., *The Papers of James Madison, Presidential Series* (Charlottesville, Va., 1984–), V, 149.

[i.e., lacks] nerve—he has not even confidence in himself ... he has been in the habit of trusting almost implicitly in Mr. Madison. Madison has acquired a complete ascendancy over him." Once again, Federalists considered Madison "as an honest man—but he was too cautious— too fearful & timid to direct the affairs of this nation." Many agreed that there was no proper leadership as the president "consulted the other heads of department but little."[177] After Madison was elected president, Jefferson only offered advice while the secretary of state—now the president-elect—made all final decisions that Jefferson clothed "with the forms of authority."[178] Repeatedly Jefferson expressed confidence in Madison as "eminently qualified as a safe depository by the endowments of integrity, understanding, and experience."[179] According to the outgoing president, his successor possessed "the purest principles of republican patriotism" and "a wisdom and foresight second to no man on earth."[180] But, throughout the last year of Jefferson's presidency, the country drifted between war and peace.

THE PRESIDENT

Because of the restrictive trade policies of the Jefferson administration, Federalists, especially in New England, gained strength both at the state and federal levels in the 1808 elections. In Connecticut the governor and the legislature rejected the Jefferson administration's request for additional legislation to "put an end to the scandalous insubordination" in not enforcing the federal embargo

177. Plumer Memorandum, April 8 and 11, 1806, p. 478.

178. Jefferson to James Monroe, Washington, January 28, 1809, H. A. Washington, ed., *The Writings of Thomas Jefferson* (9 vols., Washington, D.C., 1853–1854), V, 420.

179. Jefferson to Henry Guest, Washington, January 4, 1809, ibid., 408.

180. Jefferson to Tadeusz Kosciusko, Monticello, February 26, 1810, ibid., 508.

on commerce. Governor Jonathan Trumbull told his legislature that the federal government's Enforcement Act contained "many very extraordinary, not to say unconstitutional provisions for its execution." He called on the legislature "to devise such constitutional measures as in their wisdom may be judged proper to avert the threatening evil." The legislature, reminiscent of Madison's and Jefferson's 1798 Virginia and Kentucky resolutions, agreed that the federal act should not be enforced, stating that they had "a sense of paramount public duty . . . to abstain from any agency in the execution of measures, which are unconstitutional and despotic."[181] Madison's old friend, Virginia Federalist Henry "Lighthorse Harry" Lee advised the incoming president to separate himself from the diplomatic policies of the previous administration. "I confess I am persuaded the less you connect your administration with the last, the better your chance to do good to your country which I am sure is your sole wish & will be both your best reward and highest glory."[182]

Others, however, expected and wanted Madison to continue Jefferson's policies. The Republican committee of Essex County, New Jersey, anticipated "the same moderate, prudent, & pacific course" as Jefferson's.[183] At the opposite end of New Jersey, the Republican committee of Salem County supported the previous "system of policy characterized by wisdom and economy at home, by justice and impartiality abroad." The committee expected much of Madison.

> We trust with the utmost confidence that the powers which the constitution of the general government has allotted you will be employed for the public benefit. We entertain no apprehensions

181. *Madison Papers, Presidential Series*, I, 13.
182. Henry Lee to James Madison Baltimore, March 5, 1809, ibid., 20.
183. Newark, March 4, 1809, ibid., 18.

that you who had so distinguished a share in proposing, in forming, and in advocating the adoption of that excellent instrument would suffer it
to be injured by the unhallowed hands of its enemies. No, Sir, we remain satisfied that it will be
preserved inviolate while you are entrusted with
the exercise of the presidential functions.[184]

The oppressive policies of Britain and France on the high
seas in restraining the rights of neutrals, "forced our government to adopt such measures as we believe would have
been attended with complete success had all our Citizens
been true to their country and its laws." Even with the
rampant smuggling that violated the embargo, success
was near if we stayed the course.[185] But the situation
boiled down to a simple choice—"whether Connecticut
shall yield to the G[eneral] government, or the G[eneral]
Government yield to Connecticut."[186]

In a single paragraph in his inaugural address,
Madison outlined the goals of his administration in following the "examples of illustrious services, successfully
rendered in the most trying difficulties, by those who have
marched before me." Madison promised

To cherish peace and friendly intercourse with all
nations having correspondent disposition; to
maintain sincere neutrality towards belligerent
nations; to prefer in all cases amicable discussion
and reasonable accommodation of differences, to
a decision of them by an appeal to Arms; to
exclude foreign intrigues and foreign partialities,
so degrading to all Countries, and so baneful to

184. The Republican Committee of Salem County, New Jersey, to
James Madison, March 3, 1809, ibid., 11–12.
185. Ibid., 12.
186. Epaphras W. Bull to James Madison, Danbury, Conn.,
March 7, 1809, ibid., 27.

free ones; to foster a spirit of independence too
just to invade the rights of others, too proud to
surrender our own, too liberal to indulge unworthy prejudices ourselves, and too elevated not to
look down upon them in others; to hold the
Union of the States as the basis of their peace and
happiness; to support the Constitution, which is
the cement of the Union, as well in its limitations
as in its authorities, to respect the rights and
authorities reserved to the States and to the people, as equally incorporated with, and essential to
the success of, the general system.[187]

Despite his strong desire to avoid war, Madison,
encouraged by "warhawks" in Congress, stumbled into it.
Upset with the continued British harassment on the high
seas and with the British incitement of Indians in the
Northwest Territory, President Madison asked Congress
for a declaration of war, which a divided Congress voted
to approve on June 18, 1812. From the beginning of the
war, American military fortunes fared badly. Old and
inept generals, incompetent leadership by the President
and his cabinet, poor recruitment and communications,
and the continued strong opposition in New England
hampered the war effort. Only the navy fared well, especially on the Great Lakes. The low point of the war
occurred in 1814 when the British briefly occupied and
burned Washington, D.C., destroying many of the public
buildings including the Capitol and the President's
Mansion. A similar British assault on Baltimore failed as
the city withstood a persistent naval bombardment that
inspired Francis Scott Key to write a poem entitled "The
Star-Spangled Banner," which after being put to music

187. James Madison, Inaugural Address, Washington, March 4,
1809, ibid., 15–18. For a general overview of Madison's presidency, see
Robert A. Rutland, *The Presidency of James Madison* (Lawrence, Kan.,
1990).

became the national anthem. General Andrew Jackson's spectacular victory over the British at New Orleans in January 1815, which occurred almost two weeks after the signing of the peace treaty at Ghent, ended the war on a high note.[188]

Despite the military problems, many Americans viewed the war as successful, and for the remainder of his presidency, Madison rode a wave of patriotic fervor. Federalists, especially New Englanders who had met in a three-week antiwar convention in Hartford from December 15, 1814, to January 5, 1815, were discredited.[189] Americans had a new sense of national pride and unity.

RETIREMENT

Madison started his long retirement on March 4, 1817. For almost twenty years he busied himself reading in a wide variety of areas and collecting and arranging his papers for a posthumous publication. He rose early, had breakfast between 8:00 and 9:00, and then relaxed on the portico with family and guests, sometimes looking through a telescope at distant plantations and the mountains. For exercise, he rode his horse Liberty about the plantation. On rainy days he walked back and forth on the porch, sometimes, it was reported, even racing Dolley. He regularly kept up his correspondence, especially with Jefferson, and served on the board of visitors of the University of Virginia from 1819 and then succeeded Jefferson as rector from 1826 to 1834. In June 1824, Samuel Whitcomb, an itinerant bookseller, described the retired president.

188. For Madison and the War of 1812, see J. C. A. Stagg, *Mr. Madison's War: Politics, Diplomacy, and Warfare in the Early Republic, 1783–1830* (Princeton, N.J., 1983) and Donald R. Hickey, *The War of 1812: A Forgotten Conflict* (Urbana, Ill., 1989).

189. For the Hartford Convention, see James M. Banner, *To the Hartford Convention: The Federalists and the Origins of Party Politics in Massachusetts, 1789–1815* (New York, 1970).

Mr. Madison is not so large or so tall as myself and instead of being a cool reserved austere man, is very sociable, rather jocose, quite sprightly, and active.... [He] appears less studied, brilliant and frank but more natural, candid and profound than Mr. Jefferson. Mr. Jefferson has more imagination and passion, quicker and richer conceptions. Mr. Madison has a sound judgment, tranquil temper and logical mind. . . . Mr. Madison has nothing in his looks, gestures, expression or manners to indicate anything extraordinary in his intellect or character, but the more one converses with him, the more his excellences are developed and the better he is liked. And yet he has a quizzical, careless, almost waggish bluntness of looks and expression which is not at all prepossessing.[190]

Two years later, in his last letter to Madison, Jefferson wrote that

The friendship which has subsisted between us, now half a century, and the harmony of our political principles and pursuits, have been sources of constant happiness to me through that long period. And if I remove beyond the reach of attentions to the University [of Virginia], or beyond the bourne of life itself, as I soon must, it is a comfort to leave that institution under your care, and an assurance that it will not be wanting. It has also been a great solace to me, to believe that you are engaged in vindicating to posterity the course we have pursued for preserving to them, in all their purity, the blessings of self-government, which we had assisted too in acquiring for them. If ever the earth has beheld a system of

190. Quoted in Ketcham, *James Madison: A Biography*, 630.

administration conducted with a single and steadfast eye to the general interest and happiness of those committed to it, one which, protected by truth, can never know reproach, it is that to which our lives have been devoted. To myself you have been a pillar of support through life. Take care of me when dead, and be assured that I shall leave with you my last affections.[191]

In his will, Jefferson, as a symbol of his friendship, gave Madison his silver-hilted walking cane.[192] Madison, in turn, in his will, bequeathed this same cane to Thomas Mann Randolph, Jefferson's grandson, "in testimony of the esteem I have for him as from the knowledge I have of the place he held in the affection of his grand father."[193]

Visitors besieged Montpelier and all reported on the conviviality of the last of the Founders. According to one visitor, "He keeps alive a strong interest in passing events,"[194] and he even served in the Virginia state constitutional convention of 1829, in which he played the role of a peacemaker. Jared Sparks, the prolific nineteenth-century historian, lived the dream of any historian in spending

five delightful days at Mr. Madison's. The situation of his residence is charming. The blossoms and verdure of the trees are just springing into perfection, and the scenery, embracing a distant view of the Blue Ridge, is commanding and beau-

191. Thomas Jefferson to James Madison, Monticello, February 17, 1826, Peterson, *Jefferson: Writings*, 1515.

192. Benjamin Franklin had given his walking cane to George Washington.

193. Robert A. Rutland, ed., *James Madison and the American Nation, 1751–1836: An Encyclopedia* (New York, 1994), 285.

194. Daniel Webster to Jeremiah Mason, Washington, December 29, 1824, Charles M. Wiltse and Harold D. Moser, eds., *The Papers of Daniel Webster, Correspondence* (Hanover, N.H., 1974), I, 379.

tiful. But I have had little time for these objects.
... The intellect and memory of Mr. Madison
appear to retain all their pristine vigor. He is
peculiarly interesting in conversation, cheerful,
gay, and full of anecdote; never a prosing talker,
but sprightly, varied, fertile in his topics, and
felicitous in his descriptions and illustrations. He
seems busy in arranging his papers. While he was
in the old Congress he rarely kept copies of his
letters, though he wrote many. He has recently
succeeded in procuring nearly all the originals
from the descendants of the persons to whom he
wrote them.[195]

Throughout his latter years Madison feared for the
preservation of the Union. He denied the neo-
Antifederalist interpretation of the Constitution as a
compact in which the states had the power to nullify federal laws. In a memorandum titled "Advice to my
Country," written in 1834, Madison wrote: "The advice
nearest to my heart and deepest in my convictions is that
the Union of the States be cherished and perpetuated. Let
the open enemy to it be regarded as a Pandora with her
box opened; and the disguised one, as the Serpent creep-
ing with his deadly wiles into Paradise."[196]

As he got older, Madison's tiny handwriting got even
smaller. "In explanation of my microscopic writing, I must
remark that the older I grow, the more my stiffening fin-
gers make smaller letters, as my feet take shorter steps;
the progress in both cases being, at the same time, more
fatiguing as well as more slow."[197] His rheumatism at

195. Jared Sparks: Journal, April 23, 1830, *Virginia Magazine of
History and Biography* 60 (1952), 264.

196. Rutland, *James Madison and the American Nation*, 284.

197. Madison to James Monroe, Montpelier, April 21, 1831, *Letters
and Other Writings of James Madison* (4 vols., Philadelphia, 1867),
IV, 179.

times became crippling, and Dolley had to attend him constantly. He suffered from shortness of breath and was obliged to sit or recline for the entire day.

Edward Coles, who had served as Madison's secretary during the presidential years, remembered Madison fondly.

> In height he was about five feet six inches, of a small and delicate form, of rather a tawney complexion, bespeaking a sedentary and studious man; his hair was originally of a dark brown colour; his eyes were bluish . . . his form, features, and manner were not commanding, but his conversation exceedingly so, and few men possessed so rich a flow of language, or so great a fund of amusing anecdotes, which were made the more interesting from their being well timed and well told. His ordinary manner was simple, modest, bland, & unostentatious, retiring from the throng and cautiously refraining from doing or saying anything to make conspicuous—This made him appear a little reserved and formal. . . . [He was] the most virtuous, calm, and amiable of men; possessed of one of the purest hearts, and best tempers with which man was ever blessed. Nothing could excite or ruffle him. Under all circumstances he was collected, and ever mindful of what was due from him to others, and cautious not to wound the feelings of any one.[198]

Madison died on June 28, 1836. The entire country mourned. Comparisons were made between Madison and Jefferson. Eulogies abounded. Henry Clay, like other statesmen of the time, praised Madison as second only to Washington as "our greatest statesman and [our] first

198. Edward Coles to Hugh Blair Grigsby, December 23, 1854, Grigsby Papers, Virginia Historical Society.

political writer. *The National Intelligencer* reported that "the last of the great lights of the Revolution . . . has sunk below the horizon . . . [and] left a radiance in the firmament."[199] In writing his last letter the day before his death, Madison reflected on his "public services." He had sincerely and steadfastly cooperated "in promoting such a reconstruction of our political system as would provide for the permanent liberty and happiness of the United States; and that of the many good fruits it has produced which have well rewarded the efforts and anxieties that led to it, no one has been a more rejoicing witness than myself."[200]

199. Quoted in Ketcham, *James Madison: A Biography*, 670–71.
200. Madison to George Tucker, Montpelier, June 27, 1836, *Letters and Other Writings of James Madison*, IV, 436.

BIBLIOGRAPHY

Adair, Douglass, ed. "James Madison's Autobiography," *William and Mary Quarterly*, 3rd ser., 2 (1945), 191–209.

Banning, Lance. *Jefferson & Madison: Three Conversations from the Founding*. Madison, Wis., 1995.

_____ *The Sacred Fire of Liberty: James Madison and the Founding of the Federal Republic*. Ithaca, N.Y., 1995.

Brant, Irving. *James Madison*. 6 vols. Indianapolis, 1941–61.

Hutchinson, William T. et al., eds. *The Papers of James Madison*. Chicago and Charlottesville, 1962–.

Ketcham, Ralph. *James Madison: A Biography*. New York, 1971.

Koch, Adrienne. *Jefferson and Madison: The Great Collaboration*. New York, 1950.

Leibiger, Stuart. *Founding Friendship: George Washington, James Madison, and the Creation of the American Republic*. Charlottesville, 1999.

McCoy, Drew R. *The Last of The Fathers: James Madison and the Republican Legacy*. Cambridge, Mass., 1989.

Matthews, Richard K. *If Men Were Angels: James Madison and the Heartless Empire of Reason*. Lawrence, Kan., 1995.

Rakove, Jack N. *James Madison and the Creation of the American Republic*. New York, 2002.

Rutland, Robert A. *James Madison: The Founding Father*. New York, 1987.

_____, ed. *James Madison and the American Nation, 1751–1836: An Encyclopedia*. New York, 1994.

Transcription Policy

The transcription policies of different documentary editions have varied over the years. I have relied on the text in the printed volumes cited in this bibliography with one exception. Whenever possible I have checked and used a literal transcription of the original manuscript.